CHRISTOPH HOHL · ROSWITHA HIRZEL

Der englisch Zeiten·Trainer

Dieser Zeiten-Trainer gehört:

_____

_____

Der Dito
Das beste Lernbuch

Der Zeiten-Trainer

Christoph Hohl, Roswitha Hirzel

Illustrationen Kaspar Flück, Solothurn; Michelle Panza, Baden
Umschlag Jordy Oral, Zürich; Beat Reck, Zürich; Patrizia Villiger, Kilchberg
Lektorat Maggi Lussi Bell, Hirzel
Printed in Germany

Erhältlich im Fachhandel

Direktbestellung & Information
www.e-dito.ch; www.e-dito.de
Mailadresse info@e-dito.ch

ISBN 978-3-9521442-3-7

Inhalt

Über den englischen Zeiten-Trainer

Warum gerade Zeiten?

Zeiten sind wichtig, besonders im Englischen. Wer mit ihnen auf Kriegsfuß steht, macht leider viele Fehler. Und auch sehr störende, denn die richtige Zeitform beweist im Englischen nicht einfach Korrektheit, sondern vermittelt eine Botschaft, einen Sinn.

Der Zeiten-Trainer setzt hier an: Das komplexe englische Zeitensystem wird genau erklärt und mit fast 150 Übungen eingeschliffen, bis es sitzt. Auf jede Unit respektive Lerneinheit folgt deshalb ein Diagnose-Test mit 25 Punkten und eine gründliche Repetition aller behandelten Lerninhalte.

Das ist das Prinzip des Lerntrainings.

Wem hilft der Zeiten-Trainer?

Der Zeiten-Trainer ist der unentbehrliche Begleiter für alle, die Englisch lernen und schon etwa ein bis drei Jahre Englischunterricht genossen haben. Egal mit welchem Lehrmittel. Denn nur der Zeiten-Trainer wird der Anwendung der englischen Tenses (Zeiten) wirklich gerecht.

Der Zeiten-Trainer ist ein ausgezeichneter Brush-up-Kurs. Sie verbessern sich nicht nur in Sachen Zeitengebrauch, sondern frischen auch das Textverständnis, weitere Grammatik und den Wortschatz auf.

Wie ist der Zeiten-Trainer aufgebaut?

Das Buch ist nicht alphabetisch, sondern nach einer inneren Logik und nach didaktischen Gesichtspunkten aufgebaut. Die Zeiten werden systematisch eingeführt – nach leicht verständlichen Gesichtspunkten. Eins baut auf dem andern auf.

Natürlich können Sie den Zeiten-Trainer auch zum Nachschlagen gebrauchen. Wenn Sie nicht mehr sicher sind, wie man eine bestimmte Zeitform verwendet, so finden Sie die entsprechenden Stellen sofort mit Hilfe des Index am Ende des Buchs.

Geht es nur um Zeiten?

Nein, es geht um mehr! Wir bieten auch viele hilfreiche Ausdrücke, Verben und mehr an, wenn der Kontext dies erfordert. Das Buch richtet sich ja nicht an Sprachwissenschaftler, sondern an Menschen, die eine Sprache lernen möchten. Deshalb orientieren wir uns ganz an der Praxis. Der Stoff wird so präsentiert, dass er leicht und natürlich aufgenommen werden kann.

Tipps zur Benutzung

Von vorne nach hinten lösen!

Lösen Sie nicht beliebige Übungen, sondern arbeiten Sie im Buch von vorne nach hinten. Denn jede Unit baut auf den vorhergehenden auf. Es wird wiederholt und geübt, was früher schon erklärt und geübt wurde. Bis es sitzt. Genau in dieser Wiederholung, kombiniert mit den einfachen und präzisen Erklärungen, liegt die Stärke des Zeiten-Trainers.

Nicht zu viel aufs Mal, dafür öfter!

Arbeiten Sie oft, aber nicht allzu lange mit dem Zeiten-Trainer. Eine halbe Stunde pro Sitzung genügt durchaus.

Ganz ohne Theorie geht es nicht!

Verschaffen Sie sich auf der Seite, wo Sie arbeiten, schnell den Überblick über die Theorie. Streichen Sie an, was für Sie neu ist. Merken Sie sich die Beispiele – eventuell sogar mit einer Lernkartei. Beginnen Sie erst dann mit den Übungen. Beachten Sie auch die Tipp-Boxen. Diese helfen ausgewählte Schwierigkeiten zu beheben und sind genau auf Ihre Lernbedürfnisse zugeschnitten.

Jede Erklärung im Buch ist mit einer Ziffer versehen, damit Sie sich gut orientieren können und die Theorie-Einträge leicht finden.

Unbekannte Wörter nachschlagen!

Wer mit dem Zeiten-Trainer arbeitet, setzt nicht nur gegen 2000 Mal die richtige Zeitform ein, sondern liest auch unzählige englische Sätze. Nutzen Sie diese Gelegenheit: Setzen Sie die Zeiten nur dann ein, wenn Sie einen Satz verstehen. Schlagen Sie unbekannte Wörter im Wörterbuch nach.

Jede Übung sofort korrigieren!

Nur so erhalten Sie rechtzeitig das entscheidende Feedback. Wenn Sie nämlich einen Fehler machen, merken Sie das sofort, und Sie können ihn gezielt "verlernen". Sie werden staunen, wie schnell Sie sich verbessern. Übrigens ist das Korrigieren dank des separaten Lösungshefts äußerst einfach.

Wir wünschen Ihnen viel Spaß und Erfolg.

Verlag und Autorenteam
Schönengrund, August 2006

Unit 1

Aufwärmrunde

to be
und
there is, there are
there was, there were

Hilfsverb 'sein' _____ Auxiliary Verb 'to be'

1   Dieses englische Verb hat von allen die meisten Formen. Hier sind Gegenwart
    und Vergangenheit.

Person	Gegenwart	Vergangenheit
I	am	was
you / we / they	are	were
he / she / it	is	was

'Es gibt, da ist' _____ 'There is, there are' etc.

2   Verwenden Sie diesen unpersönlichen Ausdruck, um mitzuteilen, dass etwas
    vorhanden ist.

	Einzahl		Mehrzahl
+	There is a hotel around the corner.	+	There are 6 cinemas in the town.
−	There isn't any coffee left.	−	There aren't any eggs in the fridge.
?	Is there anyone waiting?	?	Are there any tomatoes?
−?	Isn't there any sugar?	−?	Aren't there any candles?

3   Und dasselbe in der Vergangenheit:

	Einzahl		Mehrzahl
+	There was a phone call for you.	+	There were a lot of tourists in the city.
−	There wasn't anything to do.	−	There weren't any interesting people there.
?	Was there an accident in our street?	?	Were there a lot of people at the party?
−?	Wasn't there any champagne?	−?	Weren't there any surprises for you?

1 **Which form is best? – Setzen Sie die richtige Form von *to be* ein.**

1   I _____ always happy when I see you.

2   _____ you hungry? I can make you a sandwich.

3   Marion _____n't working today. Can I give her a message?

4   _____ Roger at home?

5   Our cat Gipsy _____ very lazy. He sleeps all day.

6   Susan and Robert _____ on holiday for three weeks now.

7   Yesterday evening I _____ at the cinema.

8   Where _____ you last Saturday? I didn't see you at Jennifer's party.

9   Jeffrey _____n't at school last Tuesday.

10   Do you think this exercise _____ too easy?

2 **There is, are, was, were ... – „Es gibt". Setzen Sie die richtige Form von *to be* ein.**

1   Be careful. There _____ ice on the roads.

2   What _____ there in the fridge? – I'll have a look. Well, there _____ some sausages, but there _____ any fish.

3   _____n't there any cheese in the fridge now?

4   Yesterday, there _____ a great movie on TV. – Yes, *Broken Flowers*. Did you watch it?

5   _____ there a lot of people at Jane's wedding last Saturday?

6   I'm going to empty the mailbox and see if there _____ any letters for me.

7   It was boring at the office. There _____n't anything interesting to do. Just typing.

8   _____ there anything good on TV tonight?

9   The last night was very dark. There _____ a lot of clouds. And there _____ no moonlight.

10   There _____ someone on the phone for you. Can you take it?

Our cat Gipsy is very lazy ...

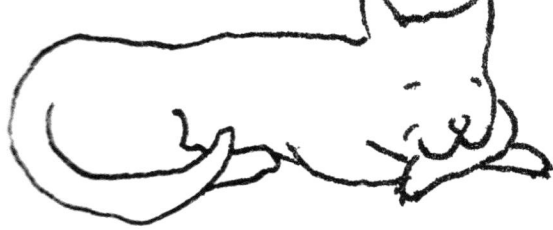

3 **Testen Sie sich. Setzen Sie *it* oder *there* ein, dazu die beste Form von *to be.***

1 I'm afraid _____ is no sugar left. …

2 … Yes, _____ / _____.

3 … _____ / _____ on the kitchen table.

4 Was _____ a sauna at the hotel where you stayed
last winter? …

5 … Yes, in fact _____ was a super wellness area.

6 Yesterday _____ / _____ an accident in our street. …

7 … Two people were hurt. _____ / _____ terrible!

8 _____ / _____ a lot of snow last week. …

9 … Yes, _____ / _____ too dangerous to go skiing …

10 … because_____ / _____ avalanches everywhere.

11 _____ / _____ so rainy last week that …

12 … _____ / _____ practically impossible to play football.

13 _____ / _____ about 50 people at Michelle's
birthday party. …

14 … _____ / _____ really a cool party!

15 Pfew! _____ / _____ extremely hot in here! …

16 … Yes, I know. _____ / _____ no air-conditioning.

17 What time _____ / _____? – 10.20. …

18 … And what's the date? – _____ / _____ the 4th.

19 How far _____ / _____ from Zurich to Munich? …

20 … _____ / _____ 230 kms.

21 _____ / _____ an unpleasant smell in here. …

22 … _____ / _____ the dog food?

23 _____ / _____ a pool at your place? …

24 … Yes, _____ / _____. …

25 … How big _____ / _____?

Unit 2

Lernen Sie die Gegenwart und ihre
Anwendung besser kennen
Present Tenses

Dazu Bedingungen Typ 0
Zero Conditional

Einfache Gegenwart ⸻⸻⸻ Present Simple

Das Present Simple ist die häufigste Zeitform im Englischen. Bilden Sie die Fragen mit do & does und die Verneinungen mit don't & doesn't.

+	I get up at 6.		+	She gets up at 6.
–	I don't get up at 6.		–	He doesn't get up at 6.
?	Do you get up at 6?		?	Does she get up at 6?
–?	Don't they get up at 6?		–?	Doesn't he get up at 6?

© Der Zeiten-Trainer, ISBN 978-3-9521442-3-7

FORMEN

- Hängen Sie in der 3. Person Einzahl, bei he, she, it, die Endung -s an.

Schreibung	Regel
wants, works	meist einfach -s anhängen
wishes, kisses	nach Zischlauten -es [iz] anhängen
try > tries, fly > flies	-y nach Konsonant wird zu -ies
stay > stays, buy > buys	-y nach Vokal aber bleibt.

4 Gewohnheiten

I always go to work at 8 o'clock.	Ich gehe immer um 8 Uhr zur Arbeit.
He doesn't usually smoke.	Er raucht gewöhnlich nicht.
Don't they sometimes sing?	Singen sie nicht manchmal?

5 Allgemeine Aussagen, was immer so ist

London has a population of 7.5m.	London hat eine Bevölkerung von 7,5 Mio.
Cooks work long hours.	Köche arbeiten viel.

6 Fahrpläne und was man nicht ändern kann

Your train leaves at 2.02.	Dein Zug fährt um 2.02.
The meeting commences at 8.	Die Versammlung beginnt um 8.

7 Zustände, Wünsche, Verben, die keine Handlung bezeichnen (statische Verben)

Do you like swimming?	Schwimmst du gerne?
They don't want to come.	Sie wollen nicht kommen.
Mary owes me £1,200.	Mary schuldet mir 1'200 Pfund.
Does Dad agree?	Ist Vater einverstanden?

→ Siehe auch Unit 6 mit einer Liste statischer Verben auf S.64.

4 **Training Gegenwart – Wählen Sie die richtige Form.**

1 Andrea often *go/goes* to work by bus because she *likes not/doesn't like* driving.

2 Nick *is/does* afraid of spiders. And Dorothy *hate/hates* mice.

3 Mr Baird just *loves/want* flying. He *flys/flies* his own airplane.

4 *Do/Does* Joan really *go/goes* to bed at 9 every evening?

5 We *aren't/don't* usually watch TV a lot.

6 *Does Mum always do/Does Mum always* the shopping?

7 Fred *go/goes* swimming twice a week. But his wife *prefer/prefers* aerobics.

8 Myriam *doesn't/isn't* always *works/work* on Saturdays.

5 **Geben Sie die Theorieziffern an** (Theorie 4–7) **und übersetzen Sie die Ausdrücke.**

1 Steht er um 7 auf?   *4*   _____

2 Mein Zug fährt um 08.15.   ___   _____

3 Sie will nicht hier bleiben. ___   _____

4 Nein. Ich rauche nicht.   ___   _____

5 Wasser kocht bei 100°.   ___   _____

6 Was fressen Pferde?   ___   _____

7 Er mag Hunde nicht.   ___   _____

8 Schuldet sie dir viel?   ___   _____

6 **Training – Verneinen Sie die Sätze.**

✓ James is happy.   _____ *James isn't happy.* _____

1 The children are at home.   _____

2 Chris wants to leave.   _____

3 Barbara wishes to see you. _____

4 Max has a shower every day. _____

5 Sue likes ice cream.   _____

6 Dad does the shopping.   _____

7 Cindy does the cleaning.   _____

Max has a shower every day.
Look! He's having a shower now!

Aktuelle Gegenwart _____ Present Continuous

Das Present Continuous besteht aus zwei Teilen, dem Hilfsverb be und dem Verb
in der -ing-Form: I'm beginning to understand.

+	I'm listening to music.	Ich höre gerade Musik.
–	You aren't listening to me.	Du hörst mir nicht zu.
?	Is she listening to him?	Hört sie ihm (jetzt) zu?
–?	Isn't he listening to the radio?	Ist er nicht gerade beim Radiohören?

FORMEN

•	Schreibung	Regel
	enjoying, working	Meist einfach –ing anhängen.
	having, making	Stummes –e (hört man nicht) fällt weg.
	dying, lying	Endung –ie wird zu –ying.
	sitting, referring	Einzelner Schlusskonsonant wird nach betontem Einzelvokal verdoppelt,
	developing, mentioning	bei unbetonter Schlusssilbe aber nicht.

8 Aktuelle Handlungen

I'm watching TV.	Ich sehe gerade fern.
Is she making coffee?	Macht sie eben Kaffee?
Isn't he doing the shopping?	Ist er nicht beim Einkaufen?

9 Für die Zukunft vereinbarte Handlungen, 'Agenda-Zukunft'

She's going to Rome *for the weekend*.	Sie geht fürs Wochenende nach Rom.
I can't come. I'm seeing the doctor *at 10*.	Ich kann nicht kommen. Ich gehe um 10 zum Arzt.
What time's Daddy coming home?	Um wie viel Uhr kommt Papa nach Hause?

→ Eine *Zeitangabe* ist notwendig.

10 Laufende Veränderungen eines Zustands

I'm getting hungry.	Ich werde (allmählich) hungrig.
You're improving.	Du machst dich (Du wirst immer besser).
We're all growing older.	Wir werden alle älter.

7 **Was fehlt? – Schreiben Sie es auf die Linie rechts.**

✓ Nicky watching TV. _____ *is* _____

1 We going to Munich at the weekend. _____

2 The kids are play in the garden. _____

3 Stella not always do her homework. _____

4 Patrick and Chris developing a new program. _____

5 I tired. I want to go home. _____

8 **Training Verlaufsform Gegenwart – Bilden Sie Sätze im *Present Continuous*.**

1 They (travel) _____ to Paris on Friday.

2 Hi Jim! What on earth (you/do) _____ here?

3 Hm. She (listen) _____ to the radio – why (she/not/do) _____ her homework?

4 It (get) _____ better and better. In fact it (develop) _____ into a real hit.

5 He is fine. He (sit) _____ here with me, (have) _____ coffee and (make) _____ all kinds of jokes.

9 **Geben Sie die Theorieziffern** (Theorie 4–10) **an und übersetzen Sie die Ausdrücke.**

1 Es wird wärmer. *10* _____

2 Nein. Ich bin am Arbeiten. __ _____

3 Mein Bus fährt um 7. __ _____

4 Ich will jetzt nicht gehen. __ _____

5 Fred fliegt morgen nach Berlin. __ _____

6 Lola steht nie vor 11 auf. __ _____

10 **Training Gegenwart – Setzen Sie *Present Simple* oder *Continuous* ein.**

1 Where (you/live) _____?

2 I (travel) _____ to Munich on 12 October.

3 How much (she/owe) _____ you?

4 Let's go home. I (get) _____ tired.

5 No, sir. This package (not contain) _____ tobacco. Well, I (not/smoke) _____.

Bedingungssätze Typ 0 _____ Zero Conditional Sentences

Zero Conditional Sentences enthalten, wie der Name sagt, eine Bedingung. Diese steht typischerweise im Nebensatz und beginnt mit dem Bindewort if (wenn, falls) oder seinem Gegenteil unless (außer, wenn nicht, es sei denn). Die hier folgenden Sätze handeln von Ursache und Wirkung.

11 Was unter einer bestimmten Bedingung immer passiert oder immer wahr ist

If you want to learn English, you need to practise.	Bedingung Hauptsatz	Wenn man Englisch lernen will, muss man üben.
You get too thin if you don't eat enough.	Hauptsatz Bedingung	Du wirst zu mager, wenn du nicht genug isst.
You don't get a coffee unless you insert a €1 coin.	Hauptsatz Bedingung	Man bekommt keinen Kaffee, wenn man keine 1€ Münze einwirft.

→ Im Englischen steht das Komma nur, wenn der Hauptsatz auf den Nebensatz folgt. Vor dem if steht also kein ~~Komma~~.

Befehl & Verbot _____ Command & Prohibition

12 Befehle mit dem einfachen Verb, Verbote mit Don't und der Grundform

Be quiet, please.	Seid bitte ruhig!
Don't think – run!	Überleg' nicht lange – lauf!
Don't worry – be happy!	Mach' dir keine Sorgen – sei glücklich!

11 Setzen Sie *if* oder *unless* ein.

1   You get no sugar _____ you press this button. Press it for sweet coffee!

2   _____ you throw a stone into water, it sinks.

3   It's hard to learn English _____ you have a good book.

4   _____ you go to China for some time, it's difficult to learn Chinese.

5   The download doesn't work _____ you click on this symbol. Click it to download!

6   _____ you heat chocolate, it melts.

7   _____ you have two hours of sunshine a day, you can heat your house with a solar unit.

12 Training Gegenwart – Wählen Sie die beste Form.

1   *Taking/Take* it easy. *Panic not/Don't panic.*

2   Now *I understand/I'm understanding* why you *tell/'re telling* me this.

3   English *gets/is getting* easier if you *practising/practise* every day.

4   Mary *sees/is seeing* the dentist next Friday.

5   *Do you like/are you liking* seafood?

6   John *has/is having* dinner at the Ritz tomorrow.

7   I *get/'m getting* thirsty. Let's go for a drink.

13 Gegenwartsformen – Setzen Sie das Richtige ein.

1   Hi, Doris. (you/enjoy) _____ the party?

2   We (develop) _____ a new package design at the moment.

3   No, Jack (not/go) _____ to the cinema very often.

4   (not/speak) _____ – just sit by my side and hold my hand.

5   Michelle always (learn) _____ the new vocabulary. And I can see that
    her German (improve) _____ now.

6   They (go) _____ to Berlin for the weekend. Their plane
    (leave) _____ at 08.15.

7   You (know) _____ the baby can't sleep (if? unless?) _____ you
    (give) _____ him his bottle.

8   What time (Pat/come) _____ home tonight?

9   Debbie (not/want) _____ to go to Dallas.

10 (Not/go) _____ out so often (if? unless?) _____ you (want)
    _____ to spend less money.

14 Testen Sie sich. Setzen Sie die besten Verbformen aus Unit 2 ein.

1 The earliest plane to Vienna (leave) _____ at 6.00.

2 (you/want) _____ a holiday? – Yes, definitely.

3 No, Barbara really (not/like) _____ oysters.

4 (children/wear) _____ school uniforms in Germany?

5 Why (you/laugh) _____ at me like this?

6 Glass (not/belong) _____ into the garbage bin.

7 Laura often (wear) _____ jeans, and …

8 … she always (look) _____ great in them.

9 Paul (not/want) _____ to see you now.

10 Just relax and (not/worry) _____!

11 Caroline! What (you/do) _____
_____ here?

12 Yes, I'm sure I (know) _____ what you mean.

13 If she (want) _____ to understand this better, …

14 … she really (need) _____ to study harder.

15 (you/prefer) _____ chicken to beef?

16 We (go) _____ to a party on Friday.

17 The game (not/work) _____ unless …

18 … you (use) _____ it with this CD rom.

19 What (Rosie/think) _____ of
our plan?

20 (not/be) _____ sad. It'll be okay.

21 She (not/believe) _____ you.

22 Now I (get) _____ hungry.

23 I still (think) _____ we should go …

24 … although it (rain) _____.

25 Excellent! My English (improve) _____.

© Der Zeiten-Trainer, ISBN 978-3-9521442-3-7

15 **Training Gegenwart – Wählen Sie die richtige Form.**

1 What are you doing out there in the kitchen? –
  I'm *making/makeing* coffee.

2 I am *refering/referring* to your boss.

3 We are *developing/developping* a new electric car.

4 He often *flys/flies* to Boston, and she often *gos/goes* to Milan.

5 Munich *has/is having* a population of about 1.2 million.

6 What time *does/is* your train *leave/leaving?*

7 The official celebration *begins/is beginning* at 10.00am.

8 Cows *don't eat/aren't eating* meat.

9 Let's stop work. I *get/am getting* tired.

10 Who *likes/does like* playing chess?

11 *Do you go/Are you going* to Berlin tomorrow?

12 *Does she like/Is she liking* Chinese food?

TIPP

Fragen
Für Fragen brauchen Sie fast immer mindestens zwei Verben:
What does he do?
Ausnahmen sind to be und Fragen nach dem Subjekt, dem ersten Wort im Satz:
Who lives here?

16 **Setzen Sie das Verb in Klammern in die richtige Form – Grundform oder *–ing*.**

1 Is Sandra still (watch) _____ TV?

2 What time do you usually (get) _____ up?

3 What are you (do) _____ tomorrow?

4 When does the train (leave) _____ for Hamburg?

5 Where do your parents (work) _____?

6 Why are you (look) _____ at me like that?

7 How does Fred (travel) _____ to work?

8 What time are you (go) _____ to the cinema tonight?

9 What do you (do) _____ for a living?

17 **Ergänzen Sie die Fragen mit *it, they* oder *there*.**

1 Why are _____ so many cars in front of the church?

2 The boys? I don't know where _____ are.

3 Is _____ anything wrong?

4 What time is _____?

5 How was Paris? Was _____ cool? – Yes, great!

6 Was _____ a lot to do at the office today?

7 Were _____ any interesting people at the party?

Revision Units 1 – 2

18 **Fragedrill – Setzen Sie *is, are, was, were, do* oder *does* in die Lücke.**

1   How _____ you today?

2   _____ Harry smoke?

3   Where _____ you going?

4   _____ the party last night a success?

5   When _____ Elaine usually get up?

6   What _____ you doing tonight?

7   That film was boring. _____ you agree?

8   _____ there any mineral water left in the cellar?

9   Why _____ n't Tom want to come?

10 How many people _____ there at the concert on Sunday?

11 Why _____ our neighbours have to work so much?

12 _____ you away last weekend?

13 Is it okay? _____ the boss agree?

14 How much _____ Tina owe you?

15 _____ you afraid of spiders?

Do you like bananas?
Martin likes bananas.

19 Training – Verneinen Sie die Sätzchen.

✓   It's raining. → *It isn't raining.*

1   Toni buys a lot of clothes.

_____

2   Ilona is at home.

_____

3   There's some milk in the fridge.

_____

4   The boss agrees.

_____

5   The children are happy here.

_____

6   There were some calls for you.

_____

7   Jeff has lunch at 1 o'clock.

_____

8   I always do the cooking.

_____

9   The baby's crying.   _____

10   Martin likes bananas.   _____

11   I'm leaving tonight.   _____

12   Jack owes you something.   _____

13   There were some letters for me.   _____

14   Swiss flies to Malta.   _____

15   I'm very hungry.   _____

16   Pat plays chess.   _____

17   Cathy does a good job.   _____

TIPP

Verneinungen
Für Verneinungen
brauchen Sie fast
immer mindestens
zwei Verben:
Joe doesn't smoke.
Die große
Ausnahme ist
to be.
(Tipp S.19: Fragen)
Vergessen Sie
nicht, dass aus
some in verneinten
Sätzen meistens
any wird.

Revision Units 1 – 2

20 **Korrigieren Sie, wenn nötig. Setzen Sie einen Haken, falls korrekt.**

1   It matters really not.   _____

2   Have you lunch at 12?   _____

3   She speaks not English.   _____

4   Tom's working in the garden.   _____

5   What does he?   _____

6   They don't always tell the truth. _____

7   No, thanks. I'm preferring water. _____

8   Yes, I realise it's a good price. _____

9   Do you afraid of the dark?   _____

10 Tell me now. I listen.   _____

11 Go not! Stay here.   _____

12 I'm really being happy.   _____

© Der Zeiten-Trainer, ISBN 978-3-9521442-3-7

21 **Training Gegenwartsformen – Übersetzen Sie.**

1   Maggie raucht gewöhnlich nicht. _____

2   Siehst du oft fern?   _____

3   Mein Zug fährt nicht um 8.   _____

4   Dan will nicht kommen.   _____

5   Du schuldest mir nichts.   _____

6   Wasser gefriert bei 0 °C.   _____

7   Bist du noch beim Arbeiten?   _____

8   Sue will mit dir sprechen.   _____

9   Ich verspreche es.   _____

10 Will dich der Chef sehen?   _____

11 Ich fahre morgen nach Zürich.   _____

12 Wann kommt Tim heute
    Abend nach Hause?   _____

13 Ich glaube, ich werde älter.   _____

14 Ich verstehe nicht.   _____

15 Findest du, es ist schön?   _____

Unit 3

Zukunftsformen
will und going to

Bedingungen
First Conditional

Zukunft mit will _____ will + infinitive

Nebst dem Gebrauch des Present Simple und Continuous für gewisse Fälle der Zukunft (Unit 2) schauen wir uns nun die beiden häufigsten Zukunftsformen an. Beginnen wir mit will und seinen verschiedenen Verwendungsmöglichkeiten.

+	John will be 20 next week.	John wird nächste Woche 20.
−	I won't forget you.	Ich werde dich nicht vergessen.
?	What will the future bring?	Was wird die Zukunft bringen?
−?	Won't you have the steak?	Nehmen sie nicht das Steak?

© Der Zeiten-Trainer, ISBN 978-3-9521442-3-7

FORMEN

• Das Will-Future wird mit will und der Grundform des Verbs gebildet. Bei der Verneinung ziehen Sie will + not in der Regel zu won't zusammen.

13 Spontane Entscheide (im Deutschen in der Gegenwart!)

I'll have the steak.   Ich *nehme* das Steak.

I'll help you with the suitcases.   Ich *helfe* dir mit den Koffern.

14 Versprechen

I'll send you an e-mail.   Ich werde dir eine E-Mail senden.

I promise I won't tell anybody.   Ich verspreche, es niemandem zu sagen.

15 Zukünftige nicht änderbare Tatsachen

Thomas will be 18 next April.   Thomas wird nächsten April 18.

16 Alles, was ungewiss oder unsicher ist

Maybe I'll open my own business in a few years.   Vielleicht werde ich in ein paar Jahren mein eigenes Geschäft eröffnen.

I hope you won't be late for our wedding!   Ich hoffe, du kommst nicht zu spät zu unserer Hochzeit!

17 Vorhersagen, welche auf subjektiver Meinung basieren

In 100 years there won't be enough oil left.   In 100 Jahren werden wir nicht mehr genug Öl haben.

Sue is great, you'll like her.   Sue ist super, du wirst sie mögen.

- "Signalwörter" – nach den folgenden Ausdrücken steht meist will:
  perhaps, maybe, probably, auch nach den Verben think, hope, expect.
- Sagen Sie, I don't think he'll buy that house, nicht: I think he won't buy that house.

22 Training Zukunft – Wählen Sie die richtige Form.

1 He probably *won't retire/retires* at 60.

2 There *willn't/won't* be enough snow to go skiing in April.

3 *Will there is/Will there be* another world war?

4 I hope he *will enjoy/will enjoys* the party.

5 I *don't think he'll/think he won't* come.

6 Waiter! I *have/'ll have* another beer, please.

23 Geben Sie die Theorieziffern an. (Theorie 13-17)

1 Susan probably won't be here tomorrow.   _____

2 We'll have the dish of the day.   _____

3 I don't think our team will win the match.   _____

4 The company will celebrate its 50th anniversary this year.   _____

5 I'll give you the money back next week.   _____

6 I won't take these shoes. They are too expensive.   _____

24 Übersetzen Sie die folgenden Sätze.

1 Ich hoffe, es schneit bald.   _____

2 Er glaubt nicht, dass sie gewinnen werden.   _____

3 Ann wird 30 nächsten Monat.   _____

4 Ich werde es nicht vergessen.   _____

5 Wird es in 50 Jahren genug
Nahrung geben?   _____
_____

6 Ich nehme den blauen Pulli.   _____

7 Ich glaube nicht, dass
ich den Wagen nehme.   _____
_____

Bedingungssätze Typ 1 _____ First Conditional Sentences

First Conditional Sentences enthalten eine Bedingung. Diese steht typischerweise im Nebensatz und beginnt mit dem Bindewort if (wenn, falls) oder seinem Gegenteil unless (außer, wenn nicht, es sei denn). Im Gegensatz zum Zero Conditional (S.16), handelt es sich beim First Conditional um eine näher definierte, konkrete Situation.

18   Was wird passieren, wenn oder falls ...

If the weather is nice,	Bedingung	Falls das Wetter schön ist,
we will go to the beach.	Hauptsatz	werden wir zum Strand gehen.
You will be happier	Hauptsatz	Du wirst glücklicher sein,
if you don't work so much.	Bedingung	wenn du nicht so viel arbeitest.
He won't get the job	Hauptsatz	Er wird die Stelle nicht kriegen,
unless he speaks English.	Bedingung	wenn er kein Englisch spricht.

→   Achtung! Der Hauptsatz steht im Futur, der Bedingungssatz im Präsens. Im normalen Bedingungssatz steht kein will. Merken Sie: if + will makes you ill.

© Der Zeiten-Trainer, ISBN 978-3-9521442-3-7

Zeit-Nebensätze _____ Time Clauses

19   when, as soon as, before

When we get home,	Zeitsatz	Wenn wir nach Hause kommen,
we will have a cup of coffee.	Hauptsatz	werden wir eine Tasse Kaffee trinken.
I will call you	Hauptsatz	Ich werde dich anrufen,
as soon as I arrive in Paris.	Zeitsatz	sobald ich in Paris ankomme.

→   Der Nebensatz, der die Zeit angibt, steht im Präsens (Gegenwart) und nicht im Futur. Das ist gleich wie im Deutschen.

WISSEN

• Signalwörter für Nebensätze, nach denen anstelle des Futurs das Präsens verwendet wird:

if	falls, wenn	as soon as	sobald
unless	es sei denn; außer	before	bevor
when	wenn, dann wann	until	bis

25 **Mehrteilige Sätze – Wählen Sie die richtige Form.**

1 If I *win/'ll win* £1 million, I *stop/'ll stop* working.

2 Unless he *works/doesn't work* more efficiently, he *loses/will lose* his job.

3 She *won't/doesn't* marry you if you *keep/will keep* flirting with other women.

4 When we*'ll get/get* to Italy, we*'ll start/start* looking for a hotel.

5 Don't forget to switch off the lights before you*'ll leave/leave* the house.

6 If we *don't catch/won't catch* this train, we*'ll take/take* the next one.

26 **Setzen Sie die richtige Verbform ein.**

1 We (not/have) _____ a picnic if it (rain) _____.

2 We (miss) _____ the plane unless we (take) _____ a taxi.

3 If you (not/arrive) _____ in time, we (leave) _____ without you.

4 When Julia (finish) _____ university, she (probably/go) _____
   _____ to Singapore for a year.

5 I (not/tell) _____ you unless you (keep) _____ it a secret.

6 If we (not/hurry) _____ , we (be) _____ late for school.

7 Marc (fail) _____ the exam unless he (study) _____ harder.

8 As soon as I (get) _____ there, I (send) _____ you an email.

27 **Übersetzen Sie.**

1 Falls er die Stelle kriegt,   _____
   wird er nach Genf ziehen.   _____

2 Was wirst du tun,   _____
   wenn er zu spät kommt?   _____

3 Ich ruf dich an,   _____
   bevor ich wegfahre.   _____

4 Wir werden den Zug verpassen,   _____
   außer wir nehmen ein Taxi.   _____

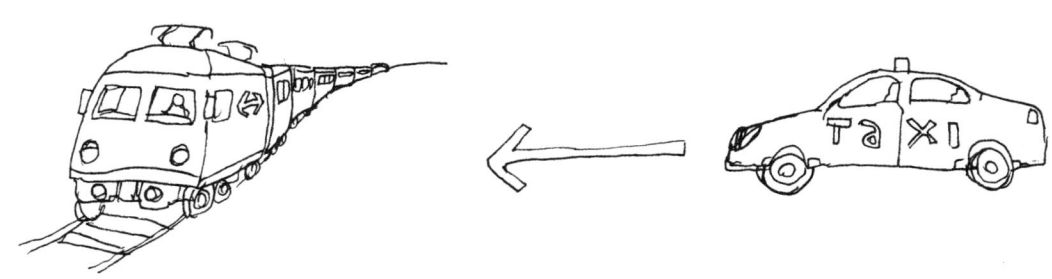

Zukunft mit 'going to' _____ be going to + infinitive

Eine weitere Form der Zukunft wird mit be + going to + Grundform des
Hauptverbs gebildet.

+	Sarah is going to drive to London.	Sarah wird nach London fahren.
–	I'm not going to invite Jim to the party.	Ich werde Jim nicht zur Party einladen.
?	When are you going to retire?	Wann wirst du in den Ruhestand treten?
–?	Isn't he going to marry her?	Wird er sie nicht heiraten?

20 Für persönliche Absichten und Pläne

I am going to learn Chinese.   Ich werde Chinesisch lernen.

What are you going to do after your   Was wirst du nach der Lehre machen?
apprenticeship?

21 Vorhersagen und Prognosen aufgrund von äußeren Anzeichen – man sieht es kommen

Look at those clouds! It's going to rain.   Schau diese Wolken an! Es wird regnen.

Sandra is going to have a baby soon.   Sandra kriegt bald ein Kind.

© Der Zeiten-Trainer, ISBN 978-3-9521442-3-7

WISSEN

- Manchmal besteht kein großer Unterschied zwischen der Zukunft mit
  going to und dem Present Continuous.
  What are you going to do tonight?   What are you doing tonight?
  I'm going to have dinner with Carla.   I'm having dinner with Carla.
- Umgangssprachlich und in Liedern hören Sie oft die Kurzversion gonna statt going to:
  I'm gonna be home tonight.

Look at those clouds!

It's going to rain.

28 **Drill – Bilden Sie Sätze mit der *going to*-Zukunft.**

1   They (get) _____ married next spring.

2   I (work) _____ on a cruise ship.

3   Look at the clear blue sky! It (not/rain) _____.

4   I (not/say) _____ anything. It's better.

5   (you/ask) _____ for a pay rise?

6   My parents (buy) _____ a Ferrari.

7   When (you/take) _____ the exam?

29 ***Will* oder *going to*? – Ergänzen Sie mit der richtigen Form und geben Sie die Theorieziffern an.** (Theorie 13-17, 20-21)

1   We _____ get married in May.   _____

2   Look at those stars! It _____ be a clear night.   _____

3   I'm not sure if Alex _____ get the job.   _____

4   What (you) _____ do after the exam?   _____

5   Soon there (not) _____ be any glaciers left.   _____

6   Wait, I _____ help you with that box.   _____

7   The Ascona Jazz Festival _____ be in June.   _____

8   No, I (not) _____ forget to post the letters.   _____

9   I expect Ann _____ win the match.   _____

10 In 2050, people _____ live on Mars.   _____

30 **An English Joke. – Setzen Sie die Verben in die richtige Zeit, *Present simple*, *will*- oder *going to-Future*.**

1   Debby: My boyfriend (be) _____ really wonderful.

2   Kate: I (agree) _____, he (seem) _____ to be very nice.

3   Debby: He (tell) _____ everybody that he (marry) _____ _____ the most beautiful girl in the world.

4   Kate: Oh, I (be) _____ sorry. But maybe he (change) _____ _____ his mind and marry you after all.

31 **Testen Sie sich. Setzen Sie für künftige Situationen die besten Zeitformen ein,
Present Simple, *will-* oder *going to-Future*.**

1   Do you know where the next summer Olympics (take) _____ place?

2   It (be) _____ my parents' wedding anniversary next week.

3   Scientists think that corral reefs (soon/die) _____.

4   He's always late. He (be) _____ late for his own funeral!

5   We (travel) _____ round the world on our honeymoon.

6   I hope we (have) _____ the chance to visit Myanmar.

7   Watch out! Snow (fall) _____ off that roof.

8   Why _____ (you/not/buy) that house?

9   I don't think Stephen (marry) _____ Sue.

10 I (make) _____ a cheese fondue
    for dinner. …

11 … Super, in that case I (cut) _____ the bread for you.

12 Susan (have) _____ a baby
    in two months.

13 We (have) _____ fish and chips, please.

14 I (not/tell)_____ anybody your secret.

15 Kevin (probably/clean) _____ the flat, …

16 … before his girlfriend (come) _____ for dinner.

17 What (you/do) _____ after school?

18 I'm sure you (like) _____ the film.

19 Maybe I (start) _____ my own duck farm …

20 … when I (be) _____ retired.

21 I (pay) _____ you back as soon as I can.

22 Unless you (work) _____ really hard,…

23 … you (not/pass) _____ this exam.

24 If you (not/speak) _____ English, …

25 … you (not/get) _____ that job.

© Der Zeiten-Trainer, ISBN 978-3-9521442-3-7

32 **Korrigieren Sie, wenn nötig. Setzen Sie einen Haken, falls korrekt.**

1   Adrian like skiing very much.   _____

2   I'm owing you £10.   _____

3   I'll call you when I'll be in London.   _____

4   My granny often rides a motorcycle.   _____

5   I think there won't be a lot of snow.   _____

6   Nadine doesn't loves Jim.   _____

7   I'm going swimming this afternoon.   _____

8   I have the steak, please.   _____

9   If I'll win €1 million, I'll buy you a car.   _____

10   He isn't agree with you.   _____

11   Be not silly!   _____

12   Jackie will have a baby soon.   _____

13   I'm going to love you forever!   _____

14   Listen! Sue plays the piano.   _____

15   I'll look after your cat while you're away.   _____

16   Does Philip has a car?   _____

17   Do you like octopus?   _____

18   There won't be any dessert unless you finish your soup.   _____

19   If you want to drive a car, you need a licence.   _____

20   We are often playing cards.   _____

33 **Training – Verneinen Sie die folgenden Sätze.**

1   John likes fish.   _____

2   We are going to Paris.   _____

3   They usually fly Lufthansa.   _____

4   I will call you.   _____

5   Peggy likes travelling.   _____

6   It's going to snow.   _____

7   There will be another war.   _____

8   If you work hard, …   _____

9   … you will pass the exam.   _____

34 Training Zukunft – Wählen Sie die beste Form, *Present Simple, Present Continuous, will* oder *going to.*

1 We (go) _____ to Locarno for the weekend.

2 I (learn) _____ Chinese in winter and, maybe someday I (start) _____ my own business in Shanghai.

3 Some people fear that in a few years there (not/be) _____ any orang-utans left.

4 The next train to London (leave) _____ at 7.15.

5 What (you/do) _____ with these apples?

6 *Four Weddings and a Funeral* (start) _____ in half an hour.

7 He (meet) _____ his boss at 2pm.

8 My uncle in Australia (be) _____ 60 next month, so I (visit) _____ him.

9 I (visit) _____ you when I (be) _____ in Paris next time.

10 She (spend) _____ the summer in a cottage in the Swiss Alps.

35 Bedingungssätze: *Zero* und *First Conditional.*

1 If we (continue) _____ destroying our planet today, we (not/have) _____ anywhere to live tomorrow.

2 You (not/get) _____ any coffee unless you (insert) _____ a €1 coin.

3 If you (heat) _____ water to 100°C, it (start) _____ boiling.

4 If I (finish) _____ work late, I (not/go) _____ to the swimming pool.

5 If you (want) _____ to drive a car, you (need) _____ a driving licence.

6 You (have) _____ to press the clutch down if you (want) _____ to change gear.

7 You (not/pass) _____ your driving test unless you (take) _____ some more lessons.

Unit 4

Lernen Sie die
Formen der Vergangenheit und deren
Verwendung besser kennen

Past Tenses
&
used to

Einfache Vergangenheit _____ Past Simple

Das Past Simple ist (nach der Gegenwart) die am zweithäufigsten verwendete Zeitform. Berichten wir von unserem letzten Urlaub oder der Party am letzten Wochenende, erzählen wir irgendeine Geschichte, meistens brauchen wir dazu die Vergangenheit.

+	He worked late last night.	Er arbeitete bis spät gestern Abend.
–	She didn't enjoy the film.	Sie genoss den Film nicht.
?	Where did you go for your holiday?	Wohin gingst du in die Ferien?
–?	Didn't you watch the game last night?	Hast du das Spiel gestern nicht angeschaut?

FORMEN

- Fügen Sie bei regelmäßigen Verben –ed oder –d an die Grundform: work – worked, like – liked.

- Ein einzelner Schlusskonsonant wird nach kurzem, betontem Vokal verdoppelt: prefer – preferred (aber develop – developed)

- Verwenden Sie für Fragen did und für Verneinungen didn't, jeweils mit der Grundform: Did you like the film? He didn't work.

- to be: I, he, she, it was (not) aber: you, we, they were (not) Bilden Sie hier die Fragen und Verneinungen direkt: were you, I wasn't, was she etc.

→ Eine Liste der unregelmäßigen Verben finden Sie im Anhang.

22 Abgeschlossene Handlungen und Zustände in der Vergangenheit

Sue didn't come to the party.	Sue kam nicht zur Party.
I had a very happy childhood.	Ich hatte eine sehr glückliche Kindheit.

23 Bei Zeitangaben der Vergangenheit sowie einer Frage danach

I met him in London in 2003.	Ich traf ihn 2003 in London.
When did you come home?	Wann kamst du nach Hause?

© Der Zeiten-Trainer, ISBN 978-3-9521442-3-7

WISSEN

- Diese Zeitangaben sind Signalwörter für das Past Tense: yesterday, ago, last (week etc.), in 2005, when, then, on 1 May, at 9am

36 **Training Vergangenheit – Wählen Sie die richtige Form.**

Last winter we **1** *goed/went/gone* to the Caribbean on a sailing trip. We **2** *flyed/flown/flew* by Air France to Martinique where we **3** *took/taked/taken* a small plane to St. Lucia. There we **4** *hire/hired/hiring* a taxi, which **5** *brings/brought/broughts* us to the marina. After some paperwork we **6** *was/are/were* ready to board the boat *Island Lady*, our home for the next two weeks. Although it **7** *rains/raineds/rained* quite often, we **8** *enjoyed/enjoyd/enjoied* our holiday very much. We **9** *didn't stay/don't stayed/stayed not* at expensive marinas but **10** *choose/chose/chosed* romantic bays, where we **11** *spended/spent/spends* the nights. Luckily, we **12** *didn't had/don't had/didn't have* any serious problems. The only drawback **13** *was/were/is* that sometimes there **14** *were/was/are* too many boats in the same place.

37 **Setzen Sie die Ausdrücke in die Vergangenheit.** (→ Verbformen im Anhang)

1   I go _____   5   he sees _____   9   we work _____

2   we feel _____   6   I am _____   10   you think _____

3   they buy_____   7   she says _____   11   he has _____

4   she is _____   8   you pay _____   12   they are _____

38 **Bilden Sie Sätze im *Past Simple*.**

1   Unfortunately, Charles (not/pass) _____ the test.
2   Where (you/be) _____ born?
3   When (you/start) _____ learning English?
4   She (spend) _____ her childhood in Puerto Rico.
5   He (go) _____ out the door and (disappear) _____ out of her life.
6   Where (Susan/meet) _____ Jeremy?
7   It was Leonardo da Vinci who (paint) _____ the Mona Lisa.
8   Rolf (not/like) _____ the show.
9   When (the film/end) _____?
10   In 2005 I (fly) _____ to New York on business.
11   (you/have) _____ a happy childhood?
12   What (the score/be) _____ in yesterday's match?

Verlaufsform der Vergangenheit _____ Past Continuous

Das Past Continuous wird für (länger) dauernde Handlungen in der Vergangenheit verwendet, die zu einem bestimmten Zeitpunkt gerade abliefen. Oft werden diese dann von kürzeren Handlungen – im Past Simple – unterbrochen oder beendet.

+	She was still working at 22.00.	Um 22.00 arbeitete sie immer noch.
–	They weren't listening to him.	Sie hörten ihm nicht zu.
?	What were you doing?	Was tatest du gerade?
–?	Wasn't he watching the film?	Schaute er sich nicht gerade den Film an?

© Der Zeiten-Trainer, ISBN 978-3-9521442-3-7

FORMEN

- Wie das Present Continuous besteht auch das Past Continuous aus zwei Teilen, dem Hilfsverb be, diesmal in der Vergangenheit, und dem Verb in der –ing–Form: I was swimming, we were working.

24   Handlungen, die zu einem bestimmten Zeitpunkt "gerade" im Gange waren

At this time last week I was lying on the beach.

Letzte Woche zu dieser Zeit lag ich am Strand.

What were you doing at 9 o'clock this morning?

Womit waren Sie heute Morgen um 9 Uhr beschäftigt?

25   Für parallel verlaufende Handlungen in der Vergangenheit

Her husband was preparing dinner while Rose was reading the newspaper.

Ihr Ehemann bereitete das Nachtessen zu, während Rose die Zeitung las.

Mr Briggs was drinking champagne at the bar while his wife was waiting for him.

Herr Briggs trank Champagner an der Bar, während seine Frau auf ihn wartete.

26   Hintergrundbeschreibungen, eine Handlung war bereits im Gange

It was raining heavily when we finally reached the cabin.

Es regnete in Strömen, als wir endlich die Hütte erreichten.

The thieves were counting the money when the police entered the room.

Die Diebe waren dabei, das Geld zu zählen, als die Polizei ins Zimmer trat.

→   Benutzen Sie für die neuen Handlungen (reached, entered) aber immer die einfache Vergangenheit (Past Simple).

39 **Setzen Sie die Sätze in die Verlaufsform der Vergangenheit (Past Continuous).**

1   Sue is singing.   _____
2   We are having a good time.   _____
3   Why aren't you listening?   _____
4   They are playing.   _____
5   What are you doing?   _____
6   Jim isn't feeling well.   _____
7   I am reading.   _____
8   What are you waiting for?   _____

40 **Wählen Sie die richtige Form.**

1   When I *woke/was waking* up this morning, it *rained/was raining*.
2   Mary *was cooking/cooked* while John *was playing/played* with the children.
3   When the bride *entered/was entering* the church, everybody *stood/was standing* up.
4   We *were driving/was driving* too fast when a police car *stopped/was stopping* us.
5   What *were you doing/did you do* at 3 o'clock yesterday afternoon?
6   The burglars *didn't look/weren't looking* pleased when the police *caught/catched* them.
7   When Lucy *came/was coming* in the room, Chris *left/was leaving* because he *didn't want/wanted not* to see her.

41 *Past Simple* oder *Continuous?* – **Setzen Sie die beste Verbform ein.**

1   When Alison (come) _____ home, Richard (sit) _____ in front of the TV.
2   We (drive) _____ round a bend when we (hit) _____ something.
3   Sharon (watch) _____ TV when the phone (ring) _____ .
4   Charlie (build) _____ a sandcastle while his sister (swim) _____ in the sea.
5   Lloyd (get) _____ up, (say) _____ good bye and (leave) _____ the room.
6   While the baby (sleep) _____ , I (relax) _____ in the bathtub.
7   Unfortunately Nancy (leave) _____ when Tony (arrive) _____ , so they only (have) _____ time for a few words.

Vergangene Gewohnheiten _____ used to + infinitive

Um vergangene Gewohnheiten oder Zustände zu beschreiben, verwenden Sie eine spezielle Konstruktion: used to + Infinitiv. Damit betont man auch, dass es jetzt nicht mehr so ist.

+	He used to be the village doctor.	Er war früher der Dorfarzt.
–	They didn't use to have a TV.	Sie hatten damals keinen Fernseher.
?	Where did you use to spend your holidays?	Wo verbrachtest du (jeweils) die Ferien?
–?	Didn't you use to work for IBM?	Hattest du nicht für IBM gearbeitet?

→ Bei der Verneinung wird häufig never verwendet: She never used to go on holiday. (Jetzt geht sie aber jeweils in die Ferien).

WISSEN

- Benutzen Sie used to für vergangene Gewohnheiten oder Zustände.
- Verwenden Sie für Zustände und Gewohnheiten in der Gegenwart die einfache Gegenwartsform: Although she doesn't work, Maggie usually gets up at 7.
- Drücken Sie einmalige frühere Aktivitäten mit der einfachen Vergangenheit aus: Joe didn't say a word, stood up and left.

27 Frühere Gewohnheiten oder Zustände – jetzt ist es anders

We used to go to Italy for our holidays.   Wir gingen stets nach Italien in die Ferien.
Did you use to travel by car?   Seid ihr (jeweils) mit dem Auto gereist?
Jean? She never used to smoke!   Jean? Sie rauchte doch früher nie!

Did you use to travel by car?

42 **Wählen Sie die bessere Form – wenn möglich mit** *(never) used to*.

1 Until I was 10, we *always spent/used to spend* our holidays at home.

2 In 2004 we *travelled/used to travel* to Italy.

3 How many hours a day did your grandfather *work/use to work?*

4 Until 2002, my parents never *went/used to go* abroad.

5 Did you *go/use to go* to school on Saturdays?

6 Once I *had/used to have* a big birthday party.

7 When I was a child, people *worked/used to work* on Saturdays.

8 My grandfather *walked/used to walk* to work.

9 1984 *was/used to be* a very happy year for me.

Bilden Sie nun inhaltlich identische Sätze mit *used to*:

10 I smoked regularly, but now I don't any longer. – I _____ .

11 Sue never wore skirts, but now she does. – Sue _____wear skirts.

12 Did you play football in the past? – Did you _____ football?

43 **Training – Verneinen Sie die folgenden Sätze.**

1 My mother used to smoke. _____

2 Martina was born in March. _____

3 Paul wrote a love letter. _____

4 At 7 o'clock I was working. _____

5 Yesterday Dad flew to Milan. _____

6 We were enjoying the party. _____

7 I spent a year in Florence. _____

44 **Bilden Sie Fragen nach dem** *kursiv* **gesetzten Ausdruck.**

✓ We went to *New York*. _____ *Where did you go?* _____

1 They got married *in 2003*. _____

2 Alice was *at home*. _____

3 I met *Jim* in London. _____

4 Carol played *the piano*. _____

5 The children were playing *Scrabble*. _____

6 Peggy used to live *in Scotland*. _____

45 **Testen Sie sich. Setzen Sie die besten Verbformen aus Unit 4 ein.**

1   When (Betty/move) _____ to Canada?

2   They (get) _____ married in Las Vegas in 2005.

3   My uncle (fly) _____ to India twice a year until he retired.

4   At this time yesterday I (sit) _____ in a bar in Paris.

5   What (you/do) _____ …

6   … when the lights (go) _____ out? …

7   … I (have) _____ a shower!

8   What (he/say) _____ …

9   … when you (tell) _____ him about
    Julia's wedding? …

10   … He (be) _____ furious.

11   In the old days people (work) _____ longer …

12   … hours and they (never/travel) _____
     _____ so much.

13   I (read) _____ the latest Harry Potter …

14   … while the kids (play) _____
     computer games.

15   In 1492 Columbus (discover) _____ America.

16   We (sail) _____ along the coast of Tahiti …

17   … when suddenly our mast (break) _____.

18   The second World War (start) _____ in 1939.

19   Last weekend there (be) _____ a lot of traffic.

20   I (dig) _____ in the garden …

21   … when I (find) _____ a Roman coin.

22   Where (you/be) _____ at this time
     yesterday?

23   When I (wake up) _____ up …

24   … this morning, it (rain) _____ .

25   As a child I (live) _____ in
     Winterthur.

© Der Zeiten-Trainer, ISBN 978-3-9521442-3-7

46 **Training Hilfsverben. Setzen Sie *am, is, are, do, does* oder *will* in die Lücke.**

1   Hello, how _____ you?

2   I _____ fine.

3   We _____ having dinner at Luigi's tonight.

4   Today _____ my father's birthday.

5   Where _____ your parents live?

6   My father _____ not work anymore.

7   I hope our team _____ win the match.

8   If she _____ not arrive soon …

9   … I _____ leave without her.

10 What exactly _____ this mean?

11 Waiter! I _____ have another glass of wine, please.

12 I _____ going to learn Tai Chi.

Vergangenheit. Setzen Sie *was, were, did, didn't* oder *used* in die Lücke.

13 Unfortunately our team _____ win.

14 Yeah, in the old days they _____ to play better.

15 We _____ watching TV when Stefano called from Boston.

16 What _____ you doing at this time yesterday? – …

17 … I _____ preparing lunch.

18 The concert last Saturday _____ a big success.

19 There _____ about 200 people there.

20 When _____ you get married?

21 As children we _____ to live in Mexico.

22 We liked it so much that we _____ want to come back.

23 Our grandparents _____ use to have a TV, but ...

24 … they _____ very happy without it.

47 Training – Verneinen Sie die folgenden Ausdrücke.

1 We like living here. _____

2 Jim wants to go home. _____

3 Do you know London? _____

4 If you learn English, _____

you'll get the job. _____

5 Kate is cleaning her flat. _____

6 They went to Canada. _____

7 Andy will write a book _____

if he has time. _____

8 Sue is going to study physics. _____

9 We used to work on Sundays. _____

10 The boss agrees. _____

11 Freddy did the dishes. _____

12 Sarah wants to become an actress. _____

48 Vervollständigen Sie den Zeitungsbericht mit *Past Simple* oder *Continuous*.

Yesterday an elderly couple (sleep) **1**_____ peacefully in their bed

when a fire (break) **2**_____ out in their apartment.

A neighbour, who (come) **3**_____ home from the pub,

(see) **4**_____ smoke coming out of their flat

and immediately (call) **5**_____ the fire brigade.

Luckily, the old people finally (wake) **6**_____ up.

They (try) **7**_____ to put out the fire

when the firemen (arrive) **8**_____.

Soon they (get) **9**_____ the fire under control

and (manage) **10**_____ to prevent it from spreading to the neighbouring flats.

Although the couple's flat (be) **11**_____ badly damaged,

they (be) **12**_____ lucky to be alive.

49 Smile – Setzen Sie die zwei fehlenden Wörter ein.

Why _____ birds fly south in winter? –

It _____ too far to walk.

50 **Training Zeitformen – Übersetzen Sie.**

1   Catherine isst nicht oft Fleisch. _____

2   Kennst du Nick? _____

3   Ich höre gerade die Nachrichten. _____

4   Ich nehme Fisch und Chips, bitte. _____

5   Was hältst du vom Hotel? _____

6   Ich glaube nicht, dass er bleibt. _____

7   Mach' das nicht! _____

8   Falls du kommst, _____
     mach' ich ein Fondue. _____

9   Morgen putze ich die Wohnung. _____

10 Karen wollte das Geld nicht. _____

11 Die Browns kauften ein Haus. _____

12 Die Gäste waren im Garten. _____

13 Warum weinst du? _____

14 Ich ruf dich an, _____
     sobald ich in Rom bin. _____

15 Kate liebt die Berge. _____

16 Thomas hat einen BMW. _____

17 Chris war beim Kochen, _____
     als das Licht ausging. _____

18 Schau, es wird gleich regnen. _____

19 Was tatest du um 7.30? _____

20 Unser Zug fährt um 17.15. _____

21 Ich glaub', ich kauf' den Hut. _____

22 Sie waren beim Schlafen, _____
     als das Feuer ausbrach. _____

23 Dein Englisch wird besser. _____

Revision Units 1 – 4

At midnight the children
were still reading …

Unit 5

Vorschläge und Wünsche
shall, let's, would like (to)

Modalverben
would, could, should

Bedingungen Typ 2
Second Conditional

Vorschlag & Wunsch _____ shall, let, would like (to)

Lernen Sie hier drei häufige Verben kennen. Sie müssen nicht verändert werden und sind im Alltag sehr nützlich und leicht zu brauchen.

28 Vorschlag, Bitte um Entscheidungshilfe – Shall ...?

Shall I call you later?	Soll ich dich später anrufen?
Shall we have fish or pizza?	Sollen wir Fisch oder Pizza essen?

29 Positiver Vorschlag – Let

Let me try this, please.	Lass' mich das versuchen, bitte!
Let's not worry about that.	Machen wir uns deswegen keine Sorgen!
Let's go out for dinner.	Gehn' wir doch aus zum Essen!

30 Konkrete Wünsche – would like, ('d like), would love etc.

How would you like to pay?	Wie möchten Sie zahlen?
I'd love to dance with you.	Ich würde sehr gern mit dir tanzen.
She'd prefer not to see you.	Sie würde es vorziehen, Sie nicht zu sehen.
We'd hate to leave now.	Wir würden jetzt gar nicht gern gehen.

→ Setzen Sie nach diesen Wünschen mit would oder der Kurzform 'd das nächste Verb in die Grundform mit to.

© Der Zeiten-Trainer, ISBN 978-3-952-1442-3-7

51 **Wählen Sie die richtige Form.**

1   *Do you like/Would you like* your boss?

2   Hot? Well, *I really like/I'd really like* to go for a swim now.

3   I'm cold. *I like/I'd like going/to go* to the sauna.

4   Good morning ma'am. *Do you like/Would you like* to read the newspaper?

5   Tricia's hobby? She really *would like/likes to travel/travelling*.

6   I'd hate *seeing/to see* you go now.

7   Shopping? No, thanks, *I prefer/I'd prefer staying/to stay* at home now.

8   We're going dancing. *Would/Do* you like *joining/to join* us?

52 *Let, shall* oder *would?* – Setzen Sie das beste Wort ein.

1 _____ me help you.

2 _____ we sit in the corner or by the window?

3 _____ you like to dance?

4 _____ I tell the boss to call you back?

5 _____ you prefer to go out for dinner?

6 Yes, _____'s listen to some music.

7 I _____ hate to fall ill now, just before my holiday.

8 _____ I get you an aspirin? – No, thanks. I'm okay.

TIPP

Why? Why not?
Benutzen Sie für einen Vorschlag oder als Reaktion auch mal diese Ausdrücke mit der Grundform.
Das ist super-easy:
Why stay at home?
Yes, why not go out?

53 Übersetzen Sie.

1 Was hält die Chefin davon? – _____

Sie schien glücklich zu sein. – _____

Ich glaube nicht, dass _____

sie einverstanden sein wird. _____

2 Möchtest du wissen, _____

wer heute Abend kommt? – _____

Spielt das eine Rolle? _____

3 Fühlst du dich gut? _____

Soll ich den Arzt anrufen? – _____

Ich würde lieber zu Bett gehen. _____

4 Bist du einverstanden? _____

5 Morgen treffe ich Mary. _____

6 Sie versprach zu kommen. _____

7 Gehen wir doch ins Kino! – _____

Ja, wieso nicht ins Kino gehen? _____

Würde, könnte, sollte _____ would, could, might & should

Mit diesen Modalverben drücken Sie etwas Nicht-Reales aus, einen Wunsch, eine Möglichkeit, Vermutung oder Verpflichtung. Diese Verben brauchen Sie auch in Verbindung mit irrealen Bedingungssätzen. → Bedingungssätze Typ 2, S. 50

31 Höfliche Bitte oder Hypothese mit 'würde'

Would you help me, please?	Würdest du mir bitte helfen?
I would never do that.	Das würde ich nie tun.
What would you do in my place?	Was würdest du an meiner Stelle tun?

32 Höfliche Bitte und Möglichkeit mit 'könnte, wäre in der Lage'

Could you sign here, please.	Könnten Sie bitte hier unterzeichnen?
Could you possibly be here by 8?	Könnten Sie vielleicht um 8 hier sein?
Chinese? I could help you.	Chinesisch? Da könnte ich dir helfen.

33 Möglichkeit mit 'könnte (eventuell), wäre allenfalls möglich'

Sue might be at home.	Sue könnte zu Hause sein.
I might go to Spain in October.	Ich gehe im Oktober vielleicht nach Spanien.

34 Annahme, Ratschlag und Verpflichtung mit 'sollte'

Billie Jean should be here soon.	Billie Jean sollte bald hier sein.
You should see a doctor at once.	Du solltest sofort zu einem Arzt gehen.
Shouldn't we go home now?	Sollten wir jetzt nicht nach Hause gehen?

© Der Zeiten-Trainer, ISBN 978-3-952-1442-3-7

WISSEN

- Das Modalverb could erfüllt zwei Funktionen:
  1 Es ist Möglichkeitsform und bedeutet könnte.
  2 Es ist Vergangenheit und bedeutet konnte. Im Zweifel verwenden Sie in der Vergangenheit *was* oder *were able to*. (→ Unit 7)

54 **Wählen Sie die richtige Form.**

1 I think you *would/should/might* be right after all.

2 I'm going to buy some lottery tickets. I *would/should/might* win a million.

3 Claire? Oh, don't worry, she *would/should/might* be home in 5 minutes.

4 If I had a lot of money, I *would/could/might* surely stop work and travel around the world.

5 I *could/should* help you further if I had more free time.

6 I'm desperate. I've lost my wedding ring and I *would/could/might* never find it again.

7 Come and watch! Joe is so fast he *would/should/might* win a medal.

8 I really think you *would/should/might* tell me the truth. – I know. But you *would/should/might* not like it.

55 **Schreiben Sie das inhaltliche Gegenteil.**

1 I have to work tonight. _____

2 You should eat a lot of sugar. _____

3 I wouldn't tell him everything. _____

4 Nancy doesn't need to be there. _____

5 You might not win anything. _____

6 Keith had to leave early. _____

7 You'll have to stay in bed. _____

© Der Zeiten-Trainer, ISBN 978-3-952-1442-3-7

56 **Training Hilfsverben. Setzen Sie *would, might, is, could, are, didn't, will* oder *don't* in die Lücke.**

1 I _____n't do my homework, and I hope the teacher _____ understand me.

2 Jim and Tina _____ really in love, _____ you agree? – Yes, absolutely. They _____ get married soon, who knows?

3 What _____ you afraid of? There _____ nothing to worry about.

4 How _____ you travel to work if you _____ have a car?

Bedingungssätze Typ 2 _____ Second Conditional

Mit dem Second Conditional kann man Bedingungen stellen oder spekulieren, was wäre, wenn ...

35   Was passieren würde, falls oder wenn

If Mary knew French, she would get the job.	Bedingung Hauptsatz	Wenn Mary Französisch könnte, bekäme sie die Stelle.
I would take a holiday if I were you.	Hauptsatz Bedingung	Ich würde Urlaub nehmen an deiner Stelle.

WISSEN

- Im Bedingungssatz wird was oft durch were ersetzt:
  If I were you, I would leave.
- Im Hauptsatz steht would + die Grundform, im Bedingungssatz die einfache Vergangenheit.
- Im Bedingungssatz steht in der Regel kein would. → 'If + would' is no good!'

57   Training Bedingungssätze – Wählen Sie die richtige Form.

1   If I *were/would be* you, I *took/would take* the job.

2   I *will/would* travel round the world if I *would have/had* enough money.

3   What *would/did* you do if you *won/would win* a lot of money?

4   I *wouldn't/didn't* trust him unless I *knew/didn't know* him better.

5   If Sam *wasn't/wouldn't be* married, his life *would be/was* easier.

6   Where *would/did* you live if you *were/would be* completely free to choose?

58   Bilden Sie Bedingungssätze Typ 2.

1   If Pete really (love) _____ Wendy, he (tell) _____ her so.

2   What (you/do) _____ if you (not/have) _____ your three children?

3   The research team (make) _____ a lot of money if they (find) _____ a cure for cancer.

4   If I (be) _____ you, I (learn) _____ the irregular verbs.

5   Joe (not/marry) _____ Jenny if she (not/be) _____ rich.

6   I (not/ask) _____ him unless I (know) _____ him well.

59 Training Zeit- und Bedingungssätze – Wählen Sie die richtige Verbform oder setzen Sie diese ein.

Typ 0

1   Press this button if you *want/will want* sugar in your coffee.

2   I'm always happy when I *see/will see* Maggie.

3   When you order very small quantities, you _____n't usually get a discount.

4   Why are we discussing this if it (not/matter) _____?

Typ 1

5   Please don't tell anyone if you *see/will see* a rat in the kitchen.

6   Ms Gray *won't/doesn't* work for you any longer unless you *pay/will pay* her more.

7   If it starts raining, we *don't/won't* go skiing at the weekend.

8   We will move house as soon as we _____ (find) a suitable place.

9   Simon won't go sailing unless the weather (get) _____ better.

10   If you (need) _____ me, I'll come to the meeting.

11   I (cook) _____ if you (do) _____ the washing-up.

Typ 2

12   The room *looked/would look* larger if we *painted/would paint* it white.

13   Yes, *I'd be/I'll be* happy to help you if I *had/would have* the time.

14   If I were you, I (see) _____ a dentist.

15   You wouldn't get into heavy traffic if you (leave) _____ earlier.

16   I'd feel safer if they finally (catch) _____ that criminal.

Alle Typen gemischt

17   If sales (not/increase) _____, we will be in trouble.

18   Would you do this if you (not/have) _____ to?

19   If you press this button, the lights (go) _____ out.

20   If the company (decide) _____ to move, I would look for another job.

21   The situation (be) _____ much better if I get a pay rise.

22   Carmen would be much healthier if she (not/smoke) _____.

23   We're going to eat in the garden if it (not/rain) _____.

24   I (tell) _____ you a good joke – if you haven't heard it before:
A lady walks up to an extremely good-looking gentleman standing at the bar in a hotel and asks, 'Excuse me, young man, do you have the time?' – 'Of course I have the time', he says, looking at her, *'if you've got the money.'*

60 **Testen Sie sich. Setzen Sie die besten Verbformen aus Unit 5 ein.**

1   _____ we dance?

2   Yes, I'd absolutely _____ to dance with you.

3   _____ you like to go skiing at the weekend?

4   Yes, great idea. _____'s do that!

5   _____ you like to pay in cash? …

6   … No, I'd _____ to pay by credit card.

7   _____ we go out tonight or stay at home and watch the game?

8   Well, why not just (stay) _____ home and watch the game?

9   You know, if I (be) _____ you,

10   … I (try) _____ to sell that car and buy a new one.

11   Buy a lottery ticket this week. You _____ win £5 million!

12   I (be) _____ lost if …

13   … I (not/have) _____ you to help me.

14   _____ you possibly drive me to the airport?

15   It (be) _____ a shame …

16   … if Chris (not/get) _____ the job.

17   You look very tired. You _____ sleep more.

18   _____ you like to go to the cinema with me tonight?

19   That suitcase _____ be too heavy for you.   …

20   … _____ me carry it.

21   _____ you like a glass of wine?

22   No idea. Ask Albert. He _____ know.

23   What _____ you (do) _____ …

24   … if you (win) _____ a lot of money?

25   If I _____ you, I'd be proud of myself.

© Der Zeiten-Trainer, ISBN 978-3-952-1442-3-7

61 **Training Hilfsverben – *aren't, isn't, wasn't, weren't, doesn't, didn't* oder *won't*?**

1   If Dick _____ love Jane anymore, why doesn't he tell her so?

2   I'm sure she _____ leave now if you ask her to stay.

3   No, your train _____ leave at 11.00 – it's 12.30, I think.

4   They couldn't drive around in that luxury car if they _____ so rich.

5   You _____ have any breakfast and you _____ hungry now? That's hard to believe!

6   Tom _____ seem to be at home, and he _____ at the office. Where is he?

7   Why _____ you looking at me? There's something wrong, _____ there?

8   No, my job _____ involve a lot of travelling now.

9   Where's Patrick? _____ you inform him about the meeting?

10 The film we saw yesterday _____ very exciting! – Yeah, I agree, I _____ like it, either.

11 I _____ tell anyone! I promise.

12 I think this English book is great. Why _____ you buy a copy for me too?

62 **Dauerbrenner 'There is' – Wählen Sie *there is, are, was, there will be* etc. oder *it is, are, was, will be* etc.**

✓   The milk? *It / is* in the fridge. – No, *there / is*n't any left.

1   I'm sure _____ / _____ / _____ cold tonight. – Yes, be careful when you drive. I think _____ / _____ / _____ ice on the roads.

2   _____ / _____ a lot of people at the party last Friday, but I still think _____ / _____ boring.

3   _____ / _____ some interesting films on TV tonight. – Yeah, but _____ / _____ late and I'm going to bed.

4   The new apartment? I promise _____ / _____ / _____ great after we renovate it. Erm, _____ / _____ / _____ many things to do before we can move in?

5   The holiday? _____ / _____ super! _____ / _____ so many things to do, _____ / _____ so much to see. _____ just _____n't enough time to do it all.

TIPP

There is, are etc.
Benutzen Sie diesen Ausdruck in allen Zeitformen, um zu sagen, dass etwas vorhanden ist, es etwas gibt:
There wasn't any music. It was boring. But there will be a good party next Friday.

Revision Units 1 – 5

63 **Training englische Zeitformen für deutsche Gegenwart – Übersetzen Sie.**

1   Wann fährt dein Zug ab?   _____

2   Was machst du heute Abend?   _____

3   Schwer? Okay, ich helfe dir.   _____

4   Mach' dir keine Sorgen. Komm'   _____
    herein. Ich mach' dir Kaffee.   _____

5   Wenn Sie Chris fragen,   _____
    hilft er Ihnen sicher.   _____

6   Was machst du gewöhnlich   _____
    an Sonntagen?   _____

7   Joe? Gestern? Ich sag's dir nicht.   _____

8   Wann beginnt die Vorstellung?   _____

9   Schöne Hose. Ich kauf' sie.   _____

10 Wenn Sie hier drücken,   _____
    bekommen Sie Kaffee.   _____

11 Es ist spät.   _____

12 Sollen wir zu Bett gehen?   _____

13 Wann stehst du morgen auf?   _____

14 Morgen fliege ich nach Ibiza.   _____

15 Ich kaufe dir ein Ticket,   _____
    wenn du willst.   _____

16 Einen Moment! Ich helfe Ihnen.   _____

Schwer? Okay, ich helfe dir ...

Halbzeit _____ Half-time

Sie haben die Hälfte des Stoffes geschafft. Die folgenden Übungen sollen Ihnen etwas Lesegenuss bieten. Have fun!

64 **Buon Appetito – wählen Sie die richtige Form.**

An Englishman **1** *would/was* visiting Rome for the first time. He **2** *stayed/was staying* at a hotel in the centre of the city. On the first morning he **3** *going/went* down to breakfast and **4** *sat/was sitting* next to an Italian. The Italian **5** *ate/was eating* a brioche (an Italian croissant) and drinking cappuccino. The Englishman **6** *ordered/was ordering* the same. When the croissants **7** *arrived/did arrive,* the Italian **8** *smiled/was smiling* and said, 'Buon appetito.'
'That **9** *must/can* be his name,' **10** *thought/was thinking* the Englishman. He **11** *smiled/used to smile* back and said his own name, 'Greengrass.'
The next morning, when Greengrass **12** *comes/came* down to breakfast again, the Italian **13** *was/were* there. 'Buon appetito,' he said again. Greengrass **14** *was/will be* a bit surprised to hear his name again, but he **15** *would reply/replied* as before, 'Greengrass.' From then on, this **16** *happened/was happening* every morning.
A few days later a friend of Greengrass's **17** *arrived/has arrived* from England.
'I'm having a wonderful time,' Mr Greengrass **18** *is saying/said.* 'I've met a very nice Italian. His name **19** *is/was* Buon Appetito.'
'That **20** *doesn't/isn't* his name,' said the friend. 'That's what Italians **21** *say/said* before they **22** *start/are* eating.'
Realizing his mistake, Greengrass **23** *ran/was running* into the restaurant. The Italian was sitting at his usual table. Greengrass sat down opposite him.
'Buon appetito!' he **24** *was shouting/shouted.*
The Italian looked at him and smiled. 'Greengrass,' he replied.

© Der Zeiten-Trainer, ISBN 978-3-952-1442-3-7

Ogden Nash (1902–1971)

My conscience

I could of
If I would of,
But I shouldn't,
So I douldn't.

Ogden Nash war lange Jahre Redaktor beim Magazin The New Yorker und
bekannt für seine Wortspielereien und witzigen bis absurden Gedichtlein.
Das Wörtchen *of* steht in diesem Gedicht über „Mein Gewissen"
an Stelle von *have* respektive *'ve* (es tönt ähnlich),
und mit *douldn't* ist *didn't* gemeint.
"Ich hätte können, wenn ich hätte wollen,
aber ich sollte nicht, deshalb tat ich nicht."

Unit 6

–ing oder nicht –ing?
Die einfachen Zeiten bei
Verben, die keine Handlung ausdrücken

Simple Tenses with Stative Verbs

Statische Verben _____ Simple Tenses with Stative Verbs

Verben drücken häufig Handlungen aus (She's walking). Das sind dynamische Verben. Statische Verben aber drücken Zustände aus (The soup tastes good), Resultate (I understand) oder Wünsche (I hope so). Und statische Verben können Sie nicht in die Continuous Form (mit –ing) setzen. Sie bleiben in den Simple Tenses. Sagen Sie: I like fish oder I don't like fish und nicht: I'm liking fish.

36 Vorliebe, Abneigung

Do you like rock music?   Magst du Rock?
He hates Brussel sprouts.   Er hasst Rosenkohl.

37 Glauben, Wissen, Denken etc.

Do you believe in God?   Glaubst du an Gott?
I agree with you.   Ich bin mit dir einverstanden.

38 Besitz, Zugehörigkeit

Does this belong here?   Gehört das hierher?
Some people have more than others.   Einige Leute besitzen mehr als andere.

39 Wünsche, Bedürfnisse

I wish you were here.   Ich wünschte, du wärest hier.
They hope to be grandparents soon.   Sie hoffen, bald Großeltern zu sein.

40 Wahrnehmung

They heard a strange noise.   Sie hörten ein seltsames Geräusch.
They don't realise the danger.   Sie erkennen die Gefahr nicht.

© Der Zeiten-Trainer, ISBN 978-3-9521442-3-7

WISSEN

- Weitere Verben, die mit dieser Bedeutung nur in den einfachen Zeiten (Simple Form) gebraucht werden:

remember	sich erinnern	seem	scheinen, aussehen als ob
forget	vergessen	appear	erscheinen
notice	merken	surprise	überraschen
promise	versprechen	mean	bedeuten
consist of	bestehen aus	depend (on)	ankommen auf, abhängen von
own	besitzen		

65 Schreiben Sie, in welche Gruppe die folgenden Verben gehören: 36–40.
Übersetzen Sie dann die Ausdrücke.

1	Does he love her?	_36_	_____
2	James knows the way.	__	_____
3	Esther didn't want to leave.	__	_____
4	I didn't recognise him.	__	_____
5	Rudi needed a new suit.	__	_____
6	We didn't have a TV.	__	_____
7	My grandma owns a Rolls.	__	_____
8	Do you prefer coffee or tea?	__	_____
9	In Alaska we saw a grizzli.	__	_____
10	Pat doesn't understand me.	__	_____

© Der Zeiten-Trainer, ISBN 978-3-9521442-3-7

66 Schreiben Sie die dritte Person Einzahl der Gegenwart. Übersetzen Sie dann die
Verben und markieren Sie jene mit ✗ , welche keine Handlung ausdrücken. Sie
sind statisch.

✓	hope	____hopes____	____hoffen____	✗
1	need	_____	_____	____
2	run	_____	_____	____
3	belong	_____	_____	____
4	wish	_____	_____	____
5	cry	_____	_____	____
6	hate	_____	_____	____
7	kiss	_____	_____	____
8	realise	_____	_____	____
9	agree	_____	_____	____
10	promise	_____	_____	____
11	hear	_____	_____	____

hope

wish

59

Bedeutungsunterschiede _____ Different Meanings

41 Einige Verben haben in einfacher und aktueller Form (–ing) andere Bedeutungen

Why are you looking at me like that?	Wieso schaust du mich so an?
You look smashing in those jeans.	In der Hose siehst du umwerfend aus.
I'm feeling fine, thanks.	Ich fühle mich gut, danke.
How do you feel about it?	Wie denkst du darüber?
What are you thinking about?	Worüber denkst du nach?
What do you think of our new boss?	Was hältst du von unserem neuen Chef?
I'm seeing June tonight.	Ich treffe June heute Abend.
I don't see your point.	Ich begreife deinen Standpunkt nicht.
The chef is tasting the soup.	Der Koch probiert die Suppe.
This Thai curry tastes delicious.	Dieser Thai Curry schmeckt köstlich.

→   Dynamischer Aspekt (Handlung mit –ing) oder statischer Gebrauch (Zustand) haben den Bedeutungsunterschied zur Folge.

67 Statisch? Dynamisch? *Present simple or continuous?* – Setzen Sie das Beste ein.

1   Today I (feel) _____ much better than yesterday.

2   What (you/think) _____ of Sue's new boyfriend?

3   I (not/see) _____ what you are trying to say.

4   Grandpa (see) _____ the doctor this afternoon.

5   This cake (taste) _____ delicious.

6   You (look) _____ wonderful tonight.

7   We (think) _____ of buying a new house.

8   How (you/feel) _____ about the result?

9   Look! Mother (taste) _____ the tomato sauce.

68 Training statisch und dynamisch – Wählen Sie die richtige Form.

1   Now I *see/am seeing* what you *mean/are meaning*.

2   The box *didn't contain/wasn't containing* anything illegal.

3   I *need/am needing* to see you today.

4   *Do you see/Are you seeing* the doctor tomorrow?

5   *Does/Is* she *wish/wishing* to see me right now?

6   The boss *wasn't agreeing/didn't agree* with my plan.

7   We *watched/were watching* TV when you *called/were calling* us.

8   I suddenly *realised/was realising* that I *travelled/was travelling* on the wrong train.

WISSEN

- Vergleichen Sie: listen – hear und look – see

  I'm listening to the radio.   I don't hear you very well.

  The visitors were looking at the painting.   They saw all the details.

  Während listen und look als Handlungen auch in der Verlaufsform vorkommen,

  ist hear und see auf die einfache Form beschränkt und bezeichnet ein Ergebnis.

69 **Gegenwart und Vergangenheit – Setzen Sie die beste Verbform ein.**

1   (you/really/mean) _____ she (not like)

    _____ shopping? I always (enjoy) _____ it.

2   (he/speak) _____ Chinese? –

    Yes, I (think) _____ so, and Thai and Korean, too.

3   I (see) _____ my uncle on TV last night.

4   The tourists (look) _____ at the signpost but couldn't read it.

5   I (not/usually/work) _____ on Saturdays. But

    this week I (substitute) _____ for the boss.

6   When (you/want) _____ to leave?

    Well, that really (depend) _____ on you.

7   On our last holiday we (stay) _____ at a very nice hotel.

    I (not/remember) _____ the name of the street, but it (be)

    _____ close to the sea.

8   He (listen) _____ to the news last night when he

    (hear) _____ a police car outside.   © Der Zeiten-Trainer, ISBN 978-3-9521442-3-7

70 **Training statische und dynamische Verben – Übersetzen Sie.**

1   Kennst du Monica?   _____

2   Ich glaube dir nicht.   _____

3   Sie hatten kein Auto.   _____

4   Heute fühl' ich mich nicht gut. _____

5   Ich brauche einen Urlaub.   _____

6   Sarah verstand mich nicht.   _____

7   Bist du einverstanden?   _____

8   Nicola liebt Bücher.   _____

9   Gestern sah Max ein UFO.   _____

10 Jetzt sieht er müde aus.   _____

71 **Testen Sie sich. Setzen Sie die besten Verbformen aus Unit 6 ein.**

1 Wow! You (look) _____ great in this dress.

2 Why (you/look) _____ at me like that?

3 Laura (not/really/like) _____ swimming.

4 You can't come? But you (promise) _____.

5 Well, I had the feeling he just (not/see) _____ our
point of view.

6 What (this product/consist) _____ of?

7 (not/worry) _____ about that too much!

8 Well, I (think) _____ of moving to Ibiza.

9 (Rosie/go) _____ to Paris next week?

10 (your boss/have) _____ a car?

11 Where's Bill? (he/not/come) _____?

12 I wonder what Neanderthal men (believe) _____ in.

13 Well, he (seem) _____ to be ill.

14 What (you/think) _____ of Kim's
new boyfriend?

15 (you/know) _____ Mary's husband?

16 That meal last night (taste) _____ wonderful.

17 What (you/do) _____ at 9pm yesterday?

18 I'm sorry, but I (not/agree) _____ with you.

19 My cat (hate) _____ the sound of violins.

20 We (sing) _____ loudly until
my neighbour knocked on the door.

21 What (you/look) _____ at?

22 I (promise) _____ I'll send
you a postcard from Naples.

23 The children (feel) _____ a
lot better today.

24 I (think) _____ he (be) _____ French.

25 I really (need) _____ a break now.

© Der Zeiten-Trainer, ISBN 978-3-9521442-3-7

72 Training Fragen – Stellen Sie die Fragen zu den kursiven Ausdrücken.

✓ Rose is sitting *in the garden*. – *Where is Rose sitting?*

1 Next week John will be *20*. – How _____ next week?

2 Cathy is *1.78*. – _____ tall _____?

3 The plane leaves *at 11.15*. – _____?

4 The boys were *playing Indians*. – _____?

5 Clive had lunch *at 12*. – What time _____ lunch?

6 Dad always says, *'Don't worry'*. – _____?

7 Cora is going to work *in Basle*. – _____?

8 We are leaving *tonight*. – _____?

9 I'm *fine*, thank you. – _____?

10 Luke wants to go *to Amsterdam*. – _____?

11 I was tired *because I worked too much*. – _____?

73 Training Hilfsverben – *am, is, are, do, does* oder *will?*

1 _____ you like roses?

2 Why _____ you laughing?

3 I hope my daughter _____ pass her exams.

4 When _____ the concert start?

5 Paul _____ listening to his MP3 player.

6 I _____ going to the Caribbean in April.

isn't, aren't, don't, doesn't oder *won't?*

7 Vegetarians _____ eat meat.

8 Luckily it _____ raining today.

9 If he _____ speak English, he _____ get the job.

10 No, we _____ going to Canada this year.

was, were, did oder *would?*

11 The burglars _____ looking for money when the police arrived.

12 What _____ you doing at this time yesterday?

13 Where _____ you use to live as a child?

14 If I were you, I _____ relax a bit more.

15 I _____ preparing dinner while my husband _____ working in the garden.

WISSEN

- Verben, die in diesen Bedeutungen NUR in der Simple Form gebraucht werden

Vorliebe, Abneigung

like	mögen, gern haben
love	lieben, sehr gern haben
hate	hassen
prefer	vorziehen, lieber haben

Wünsche, Bedürfnisse

wish	wünschen
want	wollen
hope	hoffen
need	brauchen, benötigen

Glauben, Wissen, Denken

believe	glauben
know	wissen, kennen
understand	verstehen
(dis)agree	(nicht) einverstanden sein

Besitz

belong to	gehören
possess	besitzen
own	besitzen
have	besitzen

Wahrnehmung

hear	hören
see	sehen
seem	scheinen, aussehen als ob
appear	erscheinen
realise	merken, sich im Klaren sein
notice	merken
recognise	wieder erkennen

Weitere

mean	bedeuten
promise	versprechen
forget	vergessen
remember	sich erinnern
surprise	überraschen
consist of	bestehen aus
depend (on)	ankommen auf, abhängen von

74 Training Zeitformen – Übersetzen Sie diese Repetitionssätze.

1   Ist kein Zucker da? _____

2   Es sind keine Eier
    im Kühlschrank. _____
    _____

3   Es gab einen Anruf für dich. _____

4   Er raucht gewöhnlich nicht. _____

5   Die Versammlung beginnt um 8. _____

6   Ist Vater einverstanden? _____

7   Du machst dich. _____

8   Seid bitte ruhig! _____

9   Warte! Ich helfe dir. _____

10 Ich verspreche, ich werde
    es niemandem sagen. _____

11 Ich rufe dich an, sobald ich
    in Paris eintreffe.

12 Ich habe vor, Chinesisch zu lernen.

13 Wann bist du heimgekommen?

14 Es regnete, als wir
    die Hütte erreichten.

15 Sie rauchte doch früher nie!

16 Gehn' wir doch aus zum Essen!

17 Sollen wir Fisch oder Pizza essen?

18 Wir würden jetzt gar nicht
    gern gehen.

19 Könnten Sie hier bitte
    unterzeichnen?

20 Antonieta könnte zu Hause sein.

21 Sie sollte bald hier sein.

22 Ich würde Urlaub nehmen
    an deiner Stelle *(wenn ich ...)*.

23 Gehört das hierher?

24 Ich wünschte, du wärest hier.

25 Letzte Woche zu dieser Zeit
    lag ich am Strand.

© Der Zeiten-Trainer, ISBN 978-3-9521442-3-7

Unit 7

Modalverben
must, needn't, can

… und die modalen Ausdrücke
have to, need to, be able to, be allowed to

Modalverben _____ must, needn't, mustn't, can

Modalverben geben einem Verb eine zusätzliche Bedeutung. Oft drücken sie Gewissheit aus oder Wahrscheinlichkeit, Möglichkeit oder Unmöglichkeit.

WISSEN

- Einfache Modalverben unterscheiden sich von anderen Verben:
1 Sie brauchen kein –s am Schluss anzuhängen.
2 Verneinen Sie Modalverben ganz einfach mit not.
3 In anderen Zeiten ersetzen Sie Modalverben meist durch Modale Hauptverben (zum Beispiel have to → Theorie 46).

42 Zwang, dringende Empfehlung, Folgerung oder Vermutung

Sophie must finish this before she leaves.	Sophie muss das erledigen, bevor sie geht.
We must see that film!	Den Film müssen wir sehen!
18 hours? You must be very tired!	18 Stunden? Da musst du aber müde sein!

43 Kein Zwang, keine Notwendigkeit

Max needn't worry.	Max braucht sich keine Sorgen zu machen.

44 Verbot

You mustn't tell anyone.	Du darfst (es) niemandem sagen.
We mustn't get nervous now.	Wir dürfen jetzt nicht nervös werden.

45 Fähigkeit, Bitte, Erlaubnis

I can't speak Japanese.	Ich kann nicht Japanisch.
Can you type?	Können Sie tippen?
Can I borrow your pen, please?	Darf ich mir Ihren Schreiber leihen?
Joel can use my car if he wants to.	Joel darf meinen Wagen haben, wenn er will.

© Der Zeiten-Trainer, ISBN 978-3-9521442-3-7

WISSEN

- Merken Sie sich:
1 needn't bedeutet, dass keine Notwendigkeit besteht.
2 mustn't bedeutet ein Verbot. Nicht dürfen!

75 Training Modalverben – Markieren Sie die richtigen Ausdrücke.

1 It's going to be a great game. I absolutely *can/needn't/must/could* see it.

2 Excuse me, *could/should/must* you tell me the time please?

3 I'll lock up the shop. You *can't/mustn't/needn't/couldn't* stay here till seven.

4 I'm sorry. I *shall/can't/wouldn't/mustn't* help you. It's my first visit to London too.

5 You *can/needn't/could/mustn't* say that! It's just not true!

6 Alice hasn't had lunch. She *must/needn't/mustn't/can* be very hungry.

7 This is unbelievable! Oliver *must/needn't/can't/can* speak seven languages.

8 No, really, it's okay, you *can't/mustn't/needn't/couldn't* pay for your drink.

76 Gespräch im Laden. Übersetzen Sie.

1 Guten Morgen. _____

2 Hallo. Kann ich Ihnen helfen? _____

3 Ich möchte einen Fernseher kaufen. _____

4 Was für einen Fernseher? _____

5 Ich will einen großen kaufen,
aber er darf nicht zu teuer sein. _____

6 Sie brauchen nicht den
ganzen Preis jetzt zu bezahlen. _____

7 Was meinen Sie? _____

8 Nur 50%. Den Rest können Sie
später zahlen. _____

9 Dann kann ich einen guten kaufen. _____

10 Ich kann den VIPS 916
empfehlen. Er kostet nur CHF 600. _____

11 Aber der kann nicht gut sein. _____

12 Soll ich ihn Ihnen zeigen? _____

13 Ja, sehen wir ihn doch an! _____

14 Könnten Sie hier rüber kommen? _____

  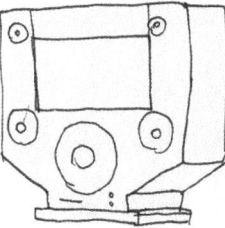

Modale Hauptverben _____ have to, need to, be able to, be allowed to

Diese Verben gleichen in ihren Bedeutungen den Modalverben, verhalten sich aber wie ganz normale Verben. Sie können sie deshalb in allen Zeiten verwenden.

46 Zwang, Notwendigkeit oder kein Zwang, keine Notwendigkeit

I'm sorry. I have to leave now.	Es tut mir Leid. Ich muss jetzt gehen.
Jim has to finish this before he leaves.	Jim muss das erledigen, bevor er geht.
Does he really have to work tomorrow?	Muss er morgen wirklich arbeiten?
Sally had to work at the weekend.	Sally musste am Wochenende arbeiten.
Why did you have to say that?	Weshalb musstest du das sagen?
I hope you won't have to go.	Ich hoffe, du wirst nicht gehen müssen.

47 Zwang, Notwendigkeit oder kein Zwang, keine Notwendigkeit

Sorry. I need to leave now.	'Tschuldigung. Ich muss jetzt gehen.
We don't need to worry.	Wir brauchen uns nicht zu sorgen.
Jim needs to finish this before he leaves.	Jim muss das erledigen, bevor er geht.
Joe doesn't need to work tomorrow.	Joe muss morgen nicht arbeiten.
Will he need to work at the weekend?	Wird er am Wochenende arbeiten müssen?

48 In der Lage sein, können

Monica wasn't able to come.	Monika konnte nicht kommen.
I'll never be able to understand that.	Das werd' ich nie verstehen können.
Will you be able to do that?	Wirst du das erledigen können?

49 Erlaubnis haben, dürfen

Jeff wasn't allowed to come.	Jeff durfte nicht kommen.
Were you allowed to leave early?	Durftest du früher weggehen?

© Der Zeiten-Trainer, ISBN 978-3-9521442-3-7

ISBN 978-3-9521442-3-7

WISSEN

- Modale Hauptverben und ihre Stellvertreter in Zeiten außer der Gegenwart:

1	must	→	had to, will have to etc.
2	needn't	→	didn't need to, didn't have to, won't need to, won't have to etc.
3	can/can't	→	was/were(n't) able to, will/won't be able to etc.
4	mustn't	→	wasn't/weren't allowed to, will/won't be allowed to etc.

77 Setzen Sie die Sätze in die Zukunft mit *will/won't* und dem modalen Hauptverb.

1 I must work today and I will _____ work tomorrow too.

2 Sorry, I can't go shopping now and I _____ to do it in the afternoon either.

3 You needn't be jealous now and you _____ never _____ be jealous, darling, because I'll always be true.

4 They now say I needn't do it, and I hope I _____ to do it any time later.

5 Her dad is so strict. She won't _____ to come with us.

6 If you inform me now, I _____ to do the job in the afternoon.

78 Setzen Sie alle Sätze in die Vergangenheit.

1 I'm sorry I wasn't able to come. I (must) _____ look after the kids.

2 (can) _____ you _____ to tell your boss what you wanted?

3 George (needn't) _____ pay a lot of taxes in Switzerland.

4 We (mustn't)_____ use Mom's car yesterday, so we (must) _____ leave at 11 to catch the last train.

5 Alison (needn't) _____ work on Friday so she (can) _____ _____ to do all the shopping for the weekend.

6 We had terrible seats. We (can't) _____ to see anything.

7 (must) _____ you _____ tell her that?

79 Training modale Verben – Übersetzen Sie.

1 Durftest du bis 2 Uhr ausgehen? _____

2 Musste Pat gestern zu Fuß gehen? _____

3 Ja, wir brauchten ein Auto. _____

4 Ich glaube nicht, (dass) ich heute werde arbeiten müssen. _____

5 Ich konnte ein Aspirin finden, ich brauchte den Arzt nicht anzurufen. _____

6 David muss jetzt zu Hause sein. _____

7 Durftest du ins Kino gehen? _____

8 Jo wird das nie vergessen können. _____

80 **Testen Sie sich. Setzen Sie die besten Verbformen aus Unit 7 ein.**

1 No food all day? You _____ be very hungry.

2 You _____ see the Rolling Stones on stage, it might be your last chance.

3 Dad's a bit strict. I don't know if I will _____ go to that party.

4 Barbara! I simply _____ call you! I've got great news.

5 I _____n't _____ to go in because I wasn't wearing a jacket.

6 Hello, this is Alice. _____ you call me back after 6 please?

7 E = mc^2? – I'll never really _____ understand that.

8 I hope I won't _____ make a speech at the meeting.

9 I'm very sorry, but I'm afraid I _____ help you.

10 Calm down. It's all right. You _____ to worry about it.

11 Sorry, darling. I _____ work until 11 o'clock yesterday.

12 No problem. I'll _____ handle the job myself.

13 Someone _____ to finish this before we go home.

14 If I won in the lottery, I might _____ to retire.

15 At the age of 17 we _____ to buy drinks.

16 If you're feeling that bad, you _____ see a doctor.

17 You _____ absolutely eat less sugar. It's not good for you.

18 I'm afraid I _____ able to go on holiday this year.

19 I had an accident. I don't think I'll ever _____ _____ to use Daddy's car again.

20 You _____ pay me back today. Take …

21 … your time, I _____ wait till next week.

22 Sorry, I won't _____ to come to your party, …

23 … I _____ be at the conference in Shanghai.

24 It's a secret. You _____ tell anyone.

25 _____ I use your pen please?

© Der Zeiten-Trainer, ISBN 978-3-9521442-3-7

81 **Training Hilfsverben – *'m, are, is, do, does, was, were* oder *did?***

1   What _____ you doing? – I _____ looking for my glasses.

2   What time _____ it? – _____ that really matter now?

3   I told Beatrice about the plan yesterday. – And _____ she agree?

4   What _____ the new boss look like? – He _____ very tall and attractive.

5   _____ your wife leaving for Florence on Friday or on Saturday?

6   What _____ you doing when I called you?

7   _____ we have to go shopping after work today?

8   _____ Nicky afraid of spiders?

9   _____ you have a red dinner jacket? – Yes. Over here. What size _____ you?

10 It _____ extremely hot yesterday, and I _____ very thirsty.

82 **Training Zukunft – Setzen Sie die beste Zeitform für künftige Handlungen ein.**

1   I (go) _____ to the cinema tonight. There's a new film.

2   June has a new boyfriend in Spain and she (learn) _____ Spanish.

3   Please don't hesitate to call me if you (have) _____ any questions.

4   The train for Cologne (leave) _____ at 08.15.

5   Do you think Sean (be) _____ at the party?

6   I (tell) _____ you as soon as I (know) _____.

7   You never know what happens. I (win) _____ 5 million in the lottery.

8   We (go) _____ swimming this afternoon unless it (rain) _____.

83 **Vergangenheit oder *used to?* – Setzen Sie ein.**

1   I (play) _____ football, but then I (hurt) _____
    my right knee and (have to) _____ give it up.

2   When I (be) _____ a boy, we _____ (have)
    chicken for dinner practically every Sunday.

3   Thank God I (stop) _____! You know I (smoke) _____
    _____ one to two packs of cigarettes a day.

4   When we (be) _____ children, we (go) _____ to
    Sunday school every weekend.   © Der Zeiten-Trainer, ISBN 978-3-9521442-3-7

© Der Zeiten-Trainer, ISBN 978-3-9521442-3-7

Revision Units 1 – 7

84 **Training Zeit im Nebensatz – Setzen Sie die beste Form ein.**

1 If Max (not/call) _____ me today, I won't be able to make a decision.

2 We wouldn't say that if we (not/be) _____ absolutely sure.

3 If you press this switch, the lights (come) _____ on.

4 I might be able to help you if I only (know) _____ what you wanted.

5 We'll go skiing unless the weather (be) _____ too bad.

6 Why don't you call me when you (be) _____ in Zurich?

7 I'll inform you as soon as I (receive) _____ their answer.

8 Karen would come with you if she (can) _____ take a week off.

85 **Welche englische Zeit wählen Sie für deutsche Gegenwart? – Übersetzen Sie.**

1 Super. Ich kaufe das Hemd. _____

2 Wann fährt der Zug nach Hamburg? _____

3 Ich bin dabei, Kaffee zu machen. _____

4 Was macht Mary in ihrer Freizeit? _____

5 Beeil' dich! Gleich regnet's! _____

6 Kommt es darauf an? _____

7 Ich hör' bald auf zu rauchen. _____

8 Wenn du das nicht versprichst, _____
werd' ich dir nichts erzählen.

86 **Training modale Verben – Übersetzen Sie.**

1 Sollen wir zum Abendessen _____
ausgehen? _____

2 Ja, weshalb nicht eine Pizza essen? _____

3 Ich möchte lieber zu Hause bleiben. _____

4 Vielleicht sind viele Leute im Kino. _____

5 Durftest du früher weggehen? _____

6 Vielleicht seh' ich dich morgen. _____

7 Lucy sollte weniger essen. _____

8 Wir möchten euch bald sehen. _____

Revision Units 1 – 7

Unit 8

Passiv in
Gegenwart, Vergangenheit, Zukunft
und bei Modalverben

Passive Voice in
Present, Past, Future
and with Modals

Grundform Passiv _____ Passive Infinitive

Beim Passiv interessiert uns weniger, wer etwas tut, als was getan wird. Die handelnde Person ist meistens unwichtig, oder wir kennen sie gar nicht. Falls wir sie aber erwähnen, fügen wir sie mit by an. Im Deutschen verwenden wir oft statt des Passivs die Konstruktion mit „man".

50 Grundform Passiv nach Modalverben

+	This book can be recommended.	Dieses Buch kann man empfehlen.
–	The departure shouldn't be delayed.	Die Abreise sollte nicht verzögert werden.
?	Will the goal be reached?	Wird das Ziel erreicht werden?
–?	Couldn't the problem be solved?	Konnte das Problem nicht gelöst werden?

51 Grundform Passiv nach Verben mit *to*

+	The boss wanted to be informed by you.	Der Chef wollte von dir informiert werden.
–	I wouldn't like to be made redundant.	Ich möchte nicht entlassen werden.
?	Is the new road going to be built soon?	Wird die neue Straße bald gebaut (werden)?
–?	Doesn't this letter have to be posted today?	Muss dieser Brief nicht heute abgeschickt werden?

© Der Zeiten-Trainer, ISBN 978-3-9521442-3-7

WISSEN

Bilden Sie das Passiv mit dem Hilfsverb be und der 3. Form des Verbs.
Die 3. Form (past participle) der regelmäßigen Verben ist die Grundform plus Endung –ed.
Nach Modalverben und going to, have to etc. steht die Grundform be und die 3. Form.

The departure shouldn't be delayed ...

87 **Drill Passiv – Ergänzen Sie mit *be* und dem Partizip des Hauptverbs.**

1   Empty bottles should (take) _____ to the bottle bank.

2   I hope Peter won't (invite) _____ to the party.

3   Can the car (pay) _____ off in monthly instalments?

4   The oven must (keep) _____ at 210°C.

5   The company would (sell) _____ if it didn't make a profit.

6   Could the cause of the fire (establish) _____?

7   If we don't change our politics, the rainforests will (destroy) _____ soon.

88 **Training Passiv – Wählen Sie die richtige Form.**

1   A concert is going to *give/be given* in aid of developing countries.

2   The books have to *return/be returned* to the library by the end of the semester.

3   Those parcels don't have to *post/be posted* until tomorrow.

4   Grandma would like to *been taken/be taken* out for dinner.

5   My printer has to *be repaired/repair*.

6   David was shy. He tried not to *see/be seen* by anyone.

7   When are these windows going to *be replaced/replace*?

89 **Übersetzen Sie. Benutzen Sie das Passiv in allen Sätzen.**

1   Billette können hier gekauft werden.   _____

2   Man wird die Fenster malen.   _____

3   Der Computer musste geprüft werden.   _____

4   Sally möchte mit dir gesehen werden.   _____

5   Autos dürfen hier nicht parkiert werden.   _____

6   Konnte die Uhr repariert werden?   _____

7   Das Hotel sollte jetzt gebucht werden.   _____

Passiv Gegenwart & Vergangenheit __ Passive Present and Past

Bilden Sie das Passiv mit dem Hilfsverb be und der 3. Form des Verbs. Setzen Sie be in die gewünschte Zeit. Passen Sie be immer dem Subjekt des Satzes an.

+	This cheese is exported.	Dieser Käse wird exportiert.
–	She wasn't promoted.	Sie wurde nicht befördert.
?	Where are these toys manufactured?	Wo werden diese Spielzeuge hergestellt?
–?	Weren't you invited to Sue's party?	Wurdest du nicht zu Sue's Fete eingeladen?

© Der Zeiten-Trainer, ISBN 978-3-9521442-3-7

52 Einfache Gegenwart – allgemein, es ist immer so

English is spoken all over the world.	Englisch wird auf der ganzen Welt gesprochen.
Coffee isn't grown in Germany.	Kaffee wird in Deutschland nicht angepflanzt.

53 Verlaufsform Gegenwart – aktuell, wird jetzt gerade gemacht

A new hotel is being built.	Man ist dabei, ein neues Hotel zu bauen.
Lots of roads are being repaired.	Zurzeit werden viele Straßen repariert.

54 Einfache Vergangenheit – wurde früher gemacht

The passengers weren't informed.	Die Passagiere wurden nicht informiert.
The thief was arrested.	Der Dieb wurde verhaftet.

55 Verlaufsform Vergangenheit – fand zum bestimmten Zeitpunkt gerade statt

Music was being played everywhere.	Überall wurde musiziert.
The rooms were being cleaned.	Die Zimmer wurden gerade gereinigt.

90 Unterstreichen Sie das Verb und geben Sie die Zeitform an.

1 Paul McCartney was born in 1942.   _____

2 Excellent cocoa is grown in Ecuador.   _____

3 A new school is being built in our town.   _____

4 Our office was being painted.   _____

5 We weren't given a pay rise.   _____

6 Where are Volvo cars produced?   _____

91 **Setzen Sie die richtige Form von *be* ein.**

1   Present Simple   Dell computers _____ assembled in Geneva.

2   Past Simple   In 2005 two baby elephants _____ born in Zurich.

3   Past Simple   The play *Romeo and Juliet* _____ written by Shakespeare.

4   Present Continuous   My car _____ serviced at the moment.

5   Past Continuous   Our TV _____ repaired so I couldn't watch the game.

6   Past Continuous   We realised that we _____ followed by a police car.

92 **How are pizzas made? – Ergänzen Sie mit dem Passiv im *Present Simple.***

1   First the dough (roll) _____ out.

2   Then the pizza base (place) _____ on an oven tray.

3   Next the tomato sauce (pour) _____ onto the pizza base.

4   Then cheese, ham and mushrooms (put) _____ on the base.

5   After that it (decorate) _____ with olives and oregano.

6   Then it (cook) _____ in the oven.

7   Afterwards the pizza (cut) _____ into slices.

8   The pizzas (serve) _____ with a salad and a glass of red wine.

93 **In a busy restaurant at midday. – Setzen Sie das *Present Continuous Passive* ein.**

Tables (lay) **1**_____ and reservations (make) **2**_____ .

Guests (welcome) **3**_____ and (show) **4**_____

to their tables. Menus (hand out) **5**_____. Food (order)

6_____ and drinks (serve) **7**_____ . Bills (write)

8_____ and money (count) **9**_____ .

94 **Training Passiv in der Vergangenheit – Wählen Sie die richtige Form.**

1   The light bulb *was/were* invented by Edison.

2   Potatoes *was/were* brought to Europe in the 16th century.

3   When I arrived, the office *was being/was been* cleaned.

4   The first radio message *was been transmitted/was transmitted* by Marconi.

5   On our way home we realised that we *were being followed/were been following.*

6   The first Lego bricks *were been produced/were produced* in Denmark.

7   We had a drink at the bar while the table *was preparing/was being prepared.*

Von Aktiv zu Passiv _____ Active-Passive Transformations

Sie können einen Aktivsatz in vier Schritten in einen Passivsatz mit dem gleichen Inhalt umformen.

56   Umwandlung aktiv zu passiv in 4 Schritten

❶   Sie nehmen das Objekt des Aktivsatzes und beginnen mit diesem Ausdruck als Subjekt den Passivsatz.

❷   Sie schauen, in welcher Zeit das Verb im Aktivsatz steht. Dann setzen Sie das Verb be in diese Zeit und stellen sicher, dass es auf das neue Subjekt abgestimmt ist.

❸   Sie finden die 3. Form des Verbs im Aktivsatz und setzen diese ein.

❹   Falls der Satz ohne den Täter oder die Täterin keinen Sinn macht, fügen Sie diese mit der Präposition by an. Häufig ist das aber unnötig.

	Subjekt	**Verb**			**Objekt**
Aktiv	❹ Agatha Christie	**wrote**			❶ the Mousetrap.
↓	Schritt ❶	Schritt ❷ ❷ Past Simple ❷ be		Schritt ❸ ❸ write ❸ 3. Form	Schritt ❹
Passiv	❶ The Mousetrap	❷ **was**		❸ **written**	❹ **by** Agatha Christie

© Der Zeiten-Trainer, ISBN 978-3-9521442-3-7

FORMEN

	Aktiv	Passiv
Present Simple	People use a lot of electricity.	A lot of electricity is used.
Present Continuous	They are servicing my car.	My car is being serviced.
Past Simple	Spielberg directed ET.	ET was directed by Spielberg.
Past Continuous	Someone was cleaning the office.	The office was being cleaned.
will-Future	People will always fight wars.	Wars will always be fought.
going to-Future	He is going to sell his house.	His house is going to be sold.

95 **Ergänzen Sie den Passivsatz mit dem Subjekt oder der handelnden Person.**

1   The police arrested the robbers.   _____ were arrested.

2   Fog delayed our flight.   Our flight was delayed _____.

3   Shakespeare wrote *Hamlet*.   _____ was written by Shakespeare.

4   Children will always enjoy stories.   Stories will always be enjoyed _____.

96 **Unterstreichen Sie das Verb im Aktivsatz und ergänzen Sie den Passivsatz.**

1   Fire destroyed the old farmhouse.
    The old farmhouse _____ by fire.

2   They won't open the new swimming pool before June.
    The new swimming pool _____ before June.

3   Someone is painting the Taylor's house.
    The Tailor's house _____.

4   The waiters were serving lunch when we arrived.
    Lunch _____ when we arrived.

5   Someone is going to design a new website for our company.
    A new website _____ for our company.

6   Do they grow rice in Thailand?
    _____ rice _____ in Thailand?

97 **Formen Sie die folgenden Sätze zu Passivsätzen um. Behalten Sie die Zeit bei.**

1   Rowan Atkinson plays Mr Bean.

    _____

2   They filmed *Gladiator* in Malta.

    _____

3   Scientists will discover a new drug for cancer.

    _____

4   They don't deliver parcels on Saturdays.

    _____

5   Look! They are advertising our product on TV!

    _____

6   They aren't going to close down the car plant.

    _____

7   Could they find a new secretary?

    _____

98 **Training Passiv – Wählen Sie die richtige Form.**

1   A charity party is going to *be given/give* to find new sponsors.

2   This DVD has to *return/be returned* to the media library within two weeks.

3   The invitation letters *don't have to be posted/haven't to post* today.

4   I wouldn't like to *been informed/be informed* like this.

5   Our car *have/has* to be serviced.

6   David is shy. He doesn't want to be *kiss/kissed* in public.

7   These windows aren't going *to be painted/to paint*.

8   Adriana wanted to *be told/tell* that she was as attractive as Miss World.

99 **Ergänzen Sie mit der richtigen Form von *be* und dem Partizip des Hauptverbs.**

1   German (speak) _____ in Austria.

2   Last week some paintings (steal) _____ from the Louvre in Paris.

3   A lot of visitors (attract) _____ to Disney World every year.

4   The Taj Mahal (build) _____ in the 17th century.

5   Afternoon tea (serve) _____ now.

6   Sandra (offer) _____ an interesting job after she left university.

7   James Bond felt he (watch) _____.

100 **Streichen Sie in folgenden Passivsätzen den Täter, falls er unnötig ist.**

1   Mandarin is spoken by most people in China.

2   Sonia's bike was stolen by someone.

3   This book was published by DITO Verlag.

4   Fiat cars are made by people in Italy.

5   The most valuable sunflowers were painted by Van Gogh.

6   The film ET was directed by Spielberg.

101 Ergänzen Sie die Passivsätze. Behalten Sie die Zeit bei.

1   Max is teaching Sue karate.

Sue _____ karate by Max.

2   IBM offered me a job.

I _____ by IBM.

3   They didn't tell Jane the truth.

Jane _____ the truth.

4   They will send you an e-mail.

You _____ an email.

5   They are showing the visitors every detail.

The visitors _____ every detail.

6   The boss promised Jack a pay rise.

Jack _____ a pay rise.

7   George gave me an iPod.

I _____ by George.

© Der Zeiten-Trainer, ISBN 978-3-9521442-3-7

> ### TIPP
>
> **Verben mit zwei Objekten**
> Hier gibt es im Englischen zwei Möglichkeiten fürs Passiv.
> **Aktiv**
> They gave Mary a gold watch.
> **Passiv unpersönlich**
> A gold watch was given to Mary.
> **Passiv persönlich**
> Mary was given a gold watch.
> (Gediegen!)

102 Training Passiv – Übersetzen Sie.

1   Diese Kleider werden in Indien gemacht.

_____

2   Radium wurde von Marie Curie entdeckt.

_____

3   Man baut gerade ein neues Fußballstadion.

_____

4   Milch kann man im Supermarkt kaufen.

_____

5   Wo wurde dieses Buch publiziert?

_____

6   Leere Flaschen sollten nicht weggeworfen werden.

_____

103 **Von aktiv zu passiv und umgekehrt. Verwenden Sie die gleiche Zeit.**

1 Tolkien wrote *Lord of the Rings. Lord of the Rings* _____ Tolkien.

2 The storm damaged a window. A window _____ the storm.

3 The employees weren't informed. They _____ the employees.

4 They were renovating the castle. The castle _____ .

5 People waste too much energy. Too much energy _____ .

6 The Olympics are watched by millions. Millions _____ the Olympics.

7 They are going to fire Mr Grey. Mr Grey _____ fired.

8 They will serve dinner at 7 p.m. Dinner _____ at 7 p.m.

9 They didn't pay for the tickets. The tickets _____ for.

10 People will always use cars. Cars _____ .

11 The police stopped us. We _____ the police.

12 They told us not to be late. We _____ not to be late.

13 VW produces many cars. Many cars _____ by VW.

14 They couldn't find the treasure. The treasure _____ .

15 People saw him at the station. He _____ at the station.

16 Computers are changing our lives.

Our lives _____ by computers.

17 Little green men won't invade our planet.

Our planet _____ little green men.

18 Coop is going to open a new branch.

A new branch _____ opened by Coop.

19 Bayer produces Aspirin.

Aspirin _____ Bayer.

20 You mustn't throw away empty batteries.

Empty batteries _____ away.

21 Has anybody told the boss? _____?

22 Will Sara be invited? _____ you _____ Sara?

23 Many shops asked them to deliver apples.

They _____ to deliver apples.

24 People grow corn in Iowa. Corn _____ in Iowa.

25 They make these pots of clay. These pots _____
_____ of clay.

104 **Writing a holiday postcard. Training – *Present Simple* oder *Continuous?***

Dear Sandy

Our trip through Alaska **1** (go) _____ very well and we **2** (enjoy) _____ this holiday a lot. We **3** (surprise) _____ by the beautiful scenery every day and most campsites **4** (be) _____ on a lake or river. Campgrounds **5** (be) _____ very big and everybody **6** (have) _____ their own fireplace. I **7** (not/like) _____ the mosquitoes. We **8** (bite) _____ every day. That sometimes **9** (make) _____ life a bit difficult. At the moment we **10** (visit) _____ Denali National Park where you can not only **11** (see) _____ a lot of wild animals but also a lot of tourists. While I **12** (write) _____ this, Phil **13** (have) _____ a beer with some people from Edmonton. Hope all **14** (be) _____ well with you.

Love
Roxanne

105 **Training Vergangenheit – Einfach oder mit *–ing?***

1   My parents (meet) _____ when they (study) _____ in Berlin.

2   While I (wait) _____ for my train, I (see) _____ my cousin, but he (not/see) _____ me.

3   We (not/get) _____ a room because they (not/have) _____ our reservation and the hotel (be) _____ full.

4   Jane (read) _____ while the boys (watch) _____ TV.

106 **Training Zukunft – Wählen Sie die richtige Form.**

1   My plane *is leaving/leaves* Zurich at 14.00.

2   Tomorrow we *will fly/are flying* to London.

3   I'm afraid Daddy *won't be/isn't being* back before dinner.

4   My grandfather *is being/will be* 90 next month.

5   Wait! *I come/I'll come* with you.

6   We hope the goods *will be delivered/are delivered* this week.

7   What *are you doing/will you do* at the weekend?

8   I think the letters *are typed/will be typed* today.

Revision Unit 1 – 8

107 Training modale Verben – Übersetzen Sie.

1 Diese Arbeit sollte heute erledigt werden.

_____

2 Könnten Sie mir die Uhrzeit sagen?

_____

3 Du musst diesen Film sehen!

_____

4 Du solltest nicht so viel arbeiten.

_____

5 Kann der Computer heute geliefert werden?

_____

6 Wir mussten eine Stunde warten.

_____

7 Du darfst nicht zu spät kommen.

_____

© Der Zeiten-Trainer, ISBN 978-3-9521442-3-7

108 Von aktiv zu passiv. Behalten Sie bei der Umwandlung die Zeitform bei.

1 Do they grow pineapples in the Bahamas?

_____

2 When did they build the Great Wall in China?

_____

3 They are going to install a new cable car in Zermatt.

_____

4 Every year they hold a boat race in Antigua.

_____

5 You can buy tickets for the jazz festival online.

_____

6 I'm not sure if we can sell all the tickets.

I'm not sure if _____

7 Look! They are serving lunch now.

Look!_____

Unit 9

Die beiden
Formen der
Vorgegenwart

Present Perfect
Simple & Continuous

Einfache Vorgegenwart _____ Present Perfect Simple

Bilden Sie das Present Perfect Simple mit have und dem Partizip des Hauptverbs, das heißt der 3. Form.

+	He has finished his work.	Er hat seine Arbeit beendet.
–	She hasn't come back yet.	Sie ist noch nicht zurückgekommen.
?	Have you heard the news?	Hast du die Neuigkeit erfahren?
–?	Haven't they gone on holiday?	Sind sie nicht in Urlaub gefahren?

WISSEN

- Bei regelmäßigen Verben fügen Sie –ed oder –d an die Grundform: work – worked, like – liked.
- Verdoppeln Sie Schlusskonsonanten, aber nur in kurzen, betonten Silben: prefer – preferred, stop – stopped (aber: develop – developed)

→   Eine Liste unregelmäßiger Verben finden Sie im Anhang.

57   Kürzlich erfolgte oder noch nicht abgeschlossene Ereignisse und Handlungen, Auswirkungen im Jetzt, Zeitpunkt der Handlung nicht erwähnt – oft mit *still, yet*

They still haven't called.	Sie haben noch immer nicht angerufen.
I can't get in. I've lost my keys.	Ich kann nicht rein. Ich hab' meine Schlüssel verloren.
Has Jim found a new job yet?	Hat Jim schon eine neue Stelle gefunden?
What a pity! They've cut down that old tree.	Wie schade, dass sie den alten Baum gefällt haben.

© Der Zeiten-Trainer, ISBN 978-3-9521442-3-7

58   Wir reden über einen Zeitraum, der noch nicht abgeschlossen ist, „dieser Tag", „mein Leben" – oft mit *ever, never*

I've written lots of mails today.	Ich hab' heute viele Mails geschrieben.
Have you ever been to New Zealand?	Bist du je in Neuseeland gewesen?
I have never seen the pyramids.	Ich habe die Pyramiden noch nie gesehen.

109 Training Vorgegenwart – Wählen Sie die richtige Form.

1 Susan *has/is* just arrived.

2 Have you *finishing/finished* your homework yet?

3 Bill *is/has* gone home.

4 We *don't have been/haven't been* to the Galapagos Islands yet.

5 They *have/are* recently been to Ibiza again.

6 Emilio still *doesn't sold/hasn't sold* his old car.

7 *Have/Has* the neighbours *moved/moving* house?

110 Drill – Bilden Sie Sätze in der einfachen Vorgegenwart.

1 Flight LX 562 (land) _____.

2 I (not/book) _____ the tickets yet.

3 I think we (meet) _____ before. – Well, actually I don't think so.

4 (you/finish) _____ your homework yet?

5 Julia (just/go) _____ to the cinema.

6 How many emails (you/write) _____ today?

7 This is the best Tandoori (I/ever/eat) _____.

8 I (not/buy) _____ any Christmas presents yet.

111 Übersetzen Sie.

1 Carol hat ein Haus gekauft. _____

2 Ich bin noch nie in Australien gewesen. _____

3 Tom hat noch keinen Job gefunden. _____

4 Sie sind gerade angekommen. _____

5 Bist du jemals in Zermatt gewesen? _____

6 Toby hat heute 20 Mails geschrieben. _____

7 Sandra ist schon nach Hause gegangen. _____

Flight LX 562 has just landed.

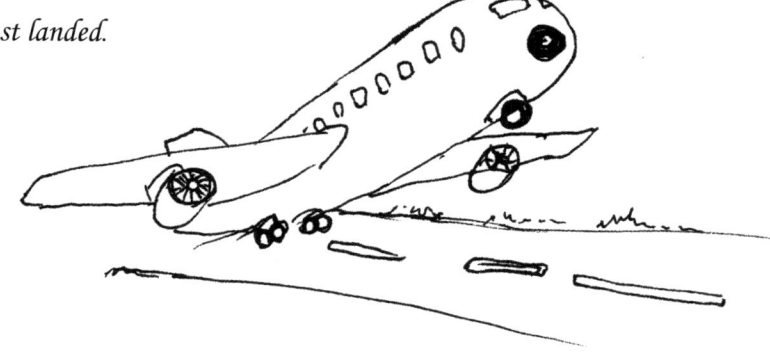

Wie lange schon? – seit _____ How long? – for, since

59 Einfache Vorgegenwart um auszudrücken, wie lange ein Zustand schon andauert – häufig mit *How long, for, since*.
Achtung, im Deutschen verwenden wir dafür die Gegenwart – oft mit „schon"!

How long have you known Nadja?	Wie lange kennst du Nadja schon?
I have known her for three years.	Ich kenne sie schon seit drei Jahren.
How long have they been married?	Wie lange sind sie schon verheiratet?
They have been married since last May.	Sie sind seit letztem Mai verheiratet.
How long has he had a Maserati?	Wie lange hat er schon einen Maserati?
He has only had it for five months.	Er hat ihn erst seit fünf Monaten.

© Der Zeiten-Trainer, ISBN 978-3-9521442-3-7

WISSEN

- Dem deutschen Wort "seit" entspricht entweder for oder since.
  Verwenden Sie for mit einer Zeitspanne:
  for one year, for two weeks, for three months, for a long time.
- Since verwenden Sie nur, wenn der Anfangspunkt genannt ist:
  since 2 o'clock, since last June, since Christmas, since I was born.

112 Drill – Ergänzen Sie mit *for* oder *since*.

1   Sibyl has lived in Paris _____ her marriage.

2   We have known each other _____ two years.

3   Karin hasn't been head of department _____ a long time.

4   William has had his Volvo _____ six months.

5   They haven't been back home _____ the war started.

6   Carl has been out of the room _____ a few minutes.

7   The musical *Cats* has been on _____ ages.

TIPP

Ein Mehrzahl -s wie bei two years weist oft auf eine Zeitspanne hin. Sagen Sie also: for two years.

113 Setzen Sie die fehlenden Wörter ein.

1   How long (you/have) _____ your new car?

2   I (have) _____ it for three months.

3   They (know) _____ each other for 20 years.

4   Sandy (live) _____ here since last March.

5   How long (they/be) _____ married?

6   Jeff (be) _____ a student since last year.

7   Ann (not/know) _____ Luca for a long time.

114 Training englische Vorgegenwart für deutsche Gegenwart – Übersetzen Sie.

1   Wie lange kennst du Kevin schon? _____

2   Ich kenne ihn seit zwei Jahren. _____

3   Wie lange ist Simona schon verheiratet? _____

4   Sie ist seit Mai verheiratet. _____

5   Wie lange sind sie schon in Perth? _____

6   Sie wohnen da seit letztem Jahr. _____

7   Ben ist noch nicht lange hier. _____

8   Wie lange hat er seine neue Stelle schon? _____

Verlaufsform der Vorgegenwart _____ Present Perfect Continuous

Verben wie learn, live, study, wait, work, die etwas länger dauernde Tätigkeiten beschreiben, werden vorzugsweise im Present Perfect Continuous verwendet.

+	He has been living here for ages.	Er lebt schon seit einer Ewigkeit hier.
–	I haven't been working for two months.	Seit zwei Monaten arbeite ich nicht.
?	How long have you been waiting?	Wie lange wartest du schon?
–?	Haven't you been learning Arabic lately?	Lernst du in letzter Zeit nicht Arabisch?

FORMEN

- Das Present Perfect Continuous besteht aus drei Teilen, dem Hilfsverb have/has + been + dem Verb in der –ing-Form:
  I have been swimming, he has been working etc.

60 Betonung der Tätigkeit, egal ob sie abgeschlossen ist oder nicht

He has been working in the garden.   Er hat im Garten gearbeitet.

Liz has been cleaning her flat.   Liz hat ihre Wohnung geputzt.

61 Ursache – Begründung eines momentanen Zustandes

I have been jogging. (That's why I'm tired.)   Ich war joggen. (Deshalb bin ich jetzt müde.)

Bryon has been repairing his car. (That's why his hands are dirty.)   Bryon hat sein Auto repariert. (Deswegen hat er schmutzige Hände.)

62 Zeitdauer einer Tätigkeit bis jetzt

I have been working for 14 hours now.   Ich arbeite jetzt schon seit 14 Stunden.

Sheila has been shopping for hours.   Sheila ist seit Stunden beim Einkaufen.

WISSEN

- Verwenden Sie aber statische Verben (like, know etc.) in der einfachen Vorgegenwart:
  She has known him for a long time. They haven't had a car since they moved to London.

115 Drill – Setzen Sie die Sätze in die Verlaufsform des Perfekts.

1 Natalie (cry) _____ .

2 We (not/enjoy) _____ ourselves.

3 Why (you/not/work) _____?

4 They (study) _____ very hard.

5 Jim (read) _____ the paper.

6 What (she/do) _____ all morning?

7 (you/wait) _____ for a long time?

116 Wählen Sie – wenn möglich – die Verlaufsform.

1 Andrea *hasn't been sleeping/hasn't slept* very well lately.

2 How long *have you been knowing/have you known* Mrs Brown?

3 We *have never been/have never been being* to New York before.

4 Simona *has been having/has had* a new car for two weeks.

5 Carol *has been losing/has lost* weight since she got her new job. She's getting slimmer and slimmer.

6 What have you *done/been doing* all morning?

7 The children *have been having/have had* a cat since last June.

© Der Zeiten-Trainer, ISBN 978-3-9521442-3-7

117 *Present Perfect Simple* oder *Continuous?*

1 Sue (not/come) _____ home yet.

2 How many cigarettes (you/smoke) _____ _____ today?

3 Adrian (drive) _____ for ten hours.

4 I (be) _____ to London several times.

5 Michelle (watch) _____ TV since 7 p.m.

6 How long (you/wait) _____?

7 I (not/write) _____ a single email today.

> **TIPP**
>
> **Tätigkeit betonen** mit Present Perfect Continuous: She has been drinking all day.
>
> **Resultat betonen** mit Present Perfect Simple: She has drunk five bottles of beer.

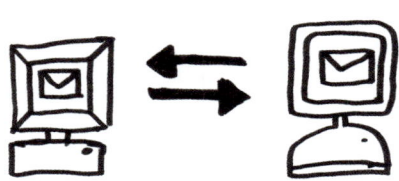

93

Vorgegenwart im Passiv _____ Present Perfect Simple Passive

63 Die Passivform der einfachen Vorgegenwart

+	All the tickets have already been sold.	Alle Tickets sind bereits verkauft.
–	Julia hasn't been invited.	Julia ist nicht eingeladen worden.
?	Has the new hospital been built yet?	Ist das neue Spital schon gebaut worden?
–?	Haven't you been informed?	Bist du nicht informiert worden?

WISSEN

- Das Passiv des Present Perfect Simple besteht aus drei Teilen,
  dem Hilfsverb have + been + past participle (3. Form) des Verbs:
  I have been informed. A new road has been built.

118 Drill Passiv – Ergänzen Sie mit der 3. Form des Verbs (Past Participle).

1 A new drug against cancer has been (find) _____.

2 Hasn't Jim been (promote) _____ recently? – Yes, he's a director now.

3 BMW cars have been (make) _____ in Germany for many years.

4 Has the local hospital already been (close) _____ down?

5 Have you been (tell) _____ about the meeting?

119 Drill Passiv – Ergänzen Sie mit der richtigen Form von *have been*.

1 The problem _____ not _____ solved yet.

2 _____ you _____ invited to the party?

3 Not many tickets _____ sold so far.

4 _____ Mary _____ sent to London?

5 Lots of chickens _____ killed by bird flu.

120 Setzen Sie die Ausdrücke in der Vorgegenwart ein.

1 A new shopping centre (build) _____ in Kensington.

2 These watches (make) _____ by an unknown company.

3 The food for the party (not/order) _____ yet.

4 (Luke/invite) _____ to Sandra's wedding?

5 (you/ever/interview) _____ by a journalist?

6 We (not/inform) _____ about the meeting yet.

121 Training Passiv – Wählen Sie die richtige Form.

1 A new perfume has been *creating/created* by Chanel.

2 How many cars *have/has* been sold by Volvo this year?

3 Gina has *given/been given* a new notebook.

4 A lot of grapes have *be/been* destroyed by the storm.

5 Some of the old skilifts *have replaced/have been replaced*.

6 Nobody has *informed/been informed* about the changes.

7 Luckily the old trees *hasn't been/haven't been* cut down.

8 All the bills *have been/have* paid.

122 Kombinieren Sie eine Satzhälfte von 1 – 7 mit einer von A – G.

1 Liana has phoned her sister   A   a long time.

2 The rent of my flat hasn't risen for   B   been done?

3 Philip has grown 5 cm since   C   every day this week.

4 He's been playing computer games   D   been doing?

5 Has the work   E   been built in the area.

6 What have you   F   I last saw him.

7 Some new houses have   G   all night.

123 Transformations – Ergänzen Sie den Passivsatz.

1 They have created a new kind of engine.

A new kind of engine _____.

2 People have known about this disease for many years.

This disease _____ about for many years.

3 They have opened a Thai restaurant in our town.

_____ in our town.

4 Has anybody posted the letters?

_____?

5 They haven't cleaned the streets yet.

_____

6 The police have already caught one of the robbers.

_____

124 Testen Sie sich. Ergänzen Sie die folgenden Vorgegenwartssätze.
Wo angegeben, benutzen Sie das Verb in Klammern.

1   How long has Audrey _____ living here?

2   They have known each other _____ seven years.

3   Martin (never/be) _____ to Los Angeles.

4   Our living room (be/redecorate) _____ .

5   How many mistakes (you/make) _____?

6   We (play) _____ games all evening.

7   He has wanted to be a doctor _____ he was a child.

8   A big tree (blow) _____ down
in the storm.

9   (you/ever/eat) _____ octopus?

10 They (sail) _____ in the …

11 … Caribbean ever _____ they gave up their jobs.

12 I (always/want) _____ to
be a farmer.

13 We (not/see) _____ each other …

14 … _____ a long time.

© Der Zeiten-Trainer, ISBN 978-3-9521442-3-7

Aktiv oder passiv? Wählen Sie die richtige Form.

15 Patricia has *known/been known* Pascal for a year.

16 A new book has *published/been published* by DITO Verlag.

17 Some of the old houses have *pulled/been pulled* down.

18 Why haven't we *informed/been informed* in time?

19 Nobody has *told/been told* me about the party.

20 The secretaries have been *typed/typing* all day.

21 The letters have been *typing/typed*.

22 Have you been *smoking/smoked*?

23 Has the salmon been *smoking/smoked*?

24 I haven't been *eating/eaten* a lot lately.

25 The cakes haven't been *eating/eaten* yet.

125 Training – Verneinen Sie die folgenden Ausdrücke.

1 I have enjoyed the concert. _____

2 Thierry usually gets up at 7. _____

3 We used to live in Oxford. _____

4 Jim will be invited. _____

5 Are you coming to the party? _____

6 Have you been shopping? _____

7 We are going to France. _____

8 Andrea is going to cook tonight. _____

9 We went to Berlin last weekend. _____

10 Our house was sold. _____

11 We had to go home. _____

12 Our car has been repaired. _____

13 Most children like spinach. _____

14 Switzerland has very dry winters. _____

126 Training Hilfsverben – Ergänzen Sie mit der richtigen Form von *be, do* oder *have*. **Manchmal benötigen Sie die verneinte Form.**

1 I _____ speak Spanish but I would like to learn it.

2 Listen! Somebody _____ playing the saxophone.

3 _____ you know Karen? She's such a sweet person.

4 My parents _____ use to travel because they _____ have the money.

5 We _____ driving too fast when the police stopped us.

6 _____ you ever been to Brazil?

7 This time last year I _____ lying on the beach getting a suntan.

8 A lot of Swiss watches _____ exported.

9 Tom is angry. He _____ _____ waiting for Carol for over an hour.

10 Unfortunately the robbers _____ _____ caught yet.

11 I asked my boss, but he _____ want to give me a pay rise, so now I _____ looking for a new job.

12 What _____ you doing tonight?

13 The kids are all dirty. They _____ _____ playing in the garden.

14 These letters can _____ posted tomorrow.

15 Where _____ you going to spend your next holiday?

127 **Setzen Sie die einfache Vorgegenwart oder die einfache Vergangenheit ein.**

1   Michelle (go) _____ shopping. She'll be back soon.

2   When (you/move) _____ to Zurich?

     We (live) _____ here since 2001.

3   (you/ever/be) _____ to China?

     Yes, I (be) _____ there six years ago.

4   How many emails (Marco/write) _____ today?

     I don't know. But yesterday he (write) _____ more than 30.

128 **Aktiv oder Passiv? – Wählen Sie die richtige Variante.**

1   You have a great view. You can *see/be seen* the Matterhorn from the hotel.

2   The job must *finish/be finished* by tomorrow.

3   Frozen pizza can *buy/be bought* in most shops and even at petrol stations.

4   He won't *give/be given* the job if he isn't prepared to speak English.

5   We are going to *open/be opened* another shop in Switzerland.

6   I would like to *take/be taken* out for dinner tonight. I don't feel like going shopping.

7   Our computers are slow. They have to *replace/be replaced*.

129 **Welche englische Zeit für deutsche Gegenwart? – Übersetzungstraining.**

1   Was möchten Sie gerne?

     _____

2   Ich nehme das Steak, bitte.

     _____

3   Heute Abend treffe ich meinen Bruder.

     _____

4   Wie lange kennst du Philip schon?

     _____

5   Ich kenne ihn seit meinem letzten Urlaub.

     _____

6   Wir warten schon seit einer Stunde auf unseren Zug.

     _____

7   Ich glaube, ich geh' nach Hause.

     _____

Unit 10

Die Vorvergangenheit
plus ein Überblick über die Erzählzeiten,
indirekte Rede und vergangene Bedingungen

Past Perfect Simple & the Narrative Tenses, Indirect Speech and Third Conditional

Einfache Vorvergangenheit _____ Past Perfect Simple

Setzen Sie ins Past Perfect Simple, was in einer Erzählung schon vor dem Erzählzeitpunkt stattgefunden hatte. Bilden Sie die Vorvergangenheit im Englischen immer mit had und der dritten Form des Verbs.

+	She had already seen the film.	Sie hatte den Film schon gesehen.
–	He still hadn't been to the office.	Er war noch nicht im Büro gewesen.
?	Where had you put the keys?	Wohin hattest du die Schlüssel gelegt?
–?	Hadn't they informed you?	Hatten sie dich nicht informiert?

→   Eine Liste der unregelmäßigen Verben finden Sie im Anhang.

Und im Passiv

+	He had already been informed.	Er war schon vorher informiert worden.
–	She hadn't been warned.	Sie war nicht gewarnt worden.
?	What had you been told?	Was war dir gesagt worden?
–?	Hadn't they been seen?	Waren sie nicht gesehen worden?

© Der Zeiten-Trainer, ISBN 978-3-9521442-3-7

64   Handlungen, die schon vor der Vergangenheit abgeschlossen waren

Sue had just left the house when Joe arrived.

Sue hatte das Haus gerade verlassen, als Joe eintraf.

We had been warned so we weren't surprised.

Wir waren gewarnt worden; deshalb waren wir nicht überrascht.

65   Zustände, die schon vor der Vergangenheit begonnen hatten

How long had you known Maggie before you got married?

Wie lange kanntest du Maggie schon, als ihr heiratetet?

Jim had owned the house for 10 years before he renovated it.

Jim hatte das Haus schon 10 Jahre, bevor er es renovierte.

130 Damals oder noch früher? – Wählen Sie die richtige Form.

1   Yesterday morning I *hadn't been able to/couldn't* find my glasses. Would you believe it, I *left/had left* them on the bus!

2   Julia *studied/had studied* the file carefully, so she *was/was been* well informed when she *had gone/went* to the meeting.

3   Unfortunately I *hadn't been/wasn't* able to accept the invitation as I *booked/had booked* a holiday at exactly that time.

4   The woman *looked/had looked* familiar to me. I *wondered/had wondered* where I *had seen/saw* her before.

5   A neighbour *was seeing/saw* the number of the car. It *was/had been* stolen two weeks before.

6   We *hadn't had/didn't have* a car at that time. We *had/had had* one for five years but then we sold it because we *were leaving/had been left* L.A. to go to New York City.

7   There *was/had been* no cake left. It *was/had been* eaten up completely.

131 Übersetzen Sie. Verwenden Sie die Vorvergangenheit.

1   Der Zug war schon abgefahren. _____

2   Sie hatten uns gewarnt. _____

3   Barbara war schon gekommen. _____

4   Eine Nachbarin hatte ihn gesehen. _____

5   Jim war vorher informiert worden. _____

6   Jane kannte Dick schon seit Jahren. _____

132 Training – Setzen Sie die Vergangenheit oder die Vorvergangenheit ein.

1   When I (want) _____ to unlock the door, I (realise) _____
    that I (lose) _____ my keys.

2   Jo (be) _____ sorry that she (not be) _____ nicer to Pat.

3   Our car (break) _____ down because it (not service) _____
    _____ for years.

4   Of course we (be) _____ surprised! No-one (tell) _____ us!

5   I (can) _____ not sleep before I (write) _____ the letter.

6   Chris (sit) _____ down to watch TV after he (do) _____
    the dishes.

7   By 2005, they (be) _____ married for 25 years.

Erzählzeiten ──────────────── Narrative Tenses

Sie kennen in der Sprache zwei Zeitensysteme: Zuerst gibt es mal das System von ‚Jetzt'; es besteht aus der Gegenwart, der Vorgegenwart und der Zukunft.
Nun wollen wir uns das System von ‚Damals' ansehen, das Sie benutzen, wenn Sie eine Geschichte erzählen, von den Ferien berichten etc.
Sie haben alle Zeiten schon gelernt, die Vergangenheit, die Vorvergangenheit und die ‚would'-Form.
Sehen Sie sich jetzt die Übersicht an.

66 Zeitenfolge in einer Geschichte – wir versetzen uns in Eveline, die im Zimmer steht und auf ihren Liebsten wartet.

It was 9 o'clock. Her suitcases were ready.	Past Simple Die Geschichte begann.	Es war 9 Uhr. Ihre Koffer standen bereit.
Eveline had met Frank just two months before. First she had just been happy to have someone to talk to, but then she had fallen in love with him.	Past Perfect Diese Handlungen waren schon vorbei, als die Geschichte begann.	Eveline hatte Frank erst vor zwei Monaten kennen gelernt. Zuerst war sie nur glücklich gewesen, dass sie jemanden hatte, mit dem sie sprechen konnte, dann hatte sie sich in ihn verliebt.
Now she was standing in her familiar old room; she was waiting for him to come and get her.	Past Continuous Hatte vorher begonnen, war noch nicht fertig.	Nun stand sie da in ihrem vertrauten alten Zimmer; sie wartete auf ihn, dass er komme und sie abhole.
She was going to leave her home and her family to go to Argentina, and they were going to get married there.	was/were going to Die Pläne für die Zukunft, von der Geschichte aus betrachtet	Sie hatte die Absicht, ihr Heim und ihre Familie zu verlassen und nach Argentinien zu gehen. Dort wollten sie heiraten.
Suddenly, there was a ring on the door, and Frank came in. She looked at him. Was it the right decision?	Past Simple Hier geht die Story weiter, eine Handlung nach der anderen.	Jetzt läutete es plötzlich an der Tür, und Frank kam herein. Sie schaute ihn an. War es die richtige Entscheidung?
Would she really be happy with him?	would Zukunft aus der Vergangenheit	Würde sie mit ihm wirklich glücklich werden? © Der Zeiten-Trainer, ISBN 978-3-9521442-3-7

→ Benutzen Sie für die neuen Handlungen immer das Past Simple (came, looked). Mit diesen aufeinander folgenden Handlungen läuft das Rad der Zeit in der Geschichte weiter.

133 Training Erzählzeiten – Markieren Sie die richtige Form.

1 Michelle *watched/was watching* figure skating when I *called/was calling* her.

2 John *hoped/had hoped* Mary *didn't/wouldn't* come. And when she *came/was coming* in, he *left/was leaving* the room immediately.

3 Tim *arrived/was arriving* at work late because he *would miss/had missed* the train.

4 Cheryl *was/had been* happy because she *finished/had finished* all her work by 4pm.

5 Monica *was buying/had bought* a Spanish book: she *would have studied/was going to study* the language so she *understood/would understand* Juan better. She *was/would be* so in love with him.

134 Erzähltraining – Setzen Sie nur die Verben in der richtigen Form auf die Linie.

1 Lilly hatte die Verabredung vergessen. (forget) _____
   Jetzt stand Tom da und wartete. (stand) _____ waiting.
   Sie hatten sich verliebt, und jetzt (fall) _____
   hatten sie die Absicht, zu heiraten; (get) _____married
   sie wussten etwas ganz sicher: (know) _____
   Sie würden immer glücklich sein. (be) _____ happy.

2 Einstein war 1879 in Ulm geboren worden. (be born) _____
   Später war er in die Schweiz gekommen. (come) _____
   Während er für das Patentamt arbeitete, (work) _____
   schrieb er die Relativitätstheorie. (write) _____
   1921 würde er den Nobelpreis erhalten. (get) _____

3 Ich war seit Jahren nicht in Peking gewesen, (be) _____
   und als ich da eintraf, (arrive) _____
   war nichts mehr so, (be) _____
   wie ich es verlassen hatte. Während ich (leave) _____
   auf dem großen Platz herumspazierte, (walk) _____
   sah ich plötzlich einen älteren Mann, der (see) _____
   mir bekannt vorkam. (seem) _____
   Es war mein alter Lehrer Ma. (be) _____
   Würde er mich noch erkennen? (recognise) _____

Indirekte Rede _____ Indirect Speech

Die indirekte Rede ist im Englischen einfacher zu bilden als im Deutschen. Am einfachsten ist dies, wenn Sie in der Gegenwart über etwas Gesagtes berichten. Dann brauchen Sie die Zeitformen in der Indirect Speech nicht zu verändern. Wurde der Bericht jedoch in der Vergangenheit gemacht, wenden Sie die folgenden einfachen Umformungsregeln an.

67 Einleitung in Gegenwart, Vorgegenwart oder Zukunft: Kein Zeitenwechsel.

"I'm in love."	He says he's in love.	Er sagt, er sei verliebt.
"We're happy."	They'll say that they're happy.	Sie werden sagen, sie seien glücklich.
"The profit has increased."	She's just said that the profit has increased.	Sie hat eben gesagt, der Profit sei gestiegen.

→ Stimmen Sie die Pronomen auf die Situation ab (I wird he oder she, we wird they).

68 Einleitung in Vergangenheit: *Present* wird zu *Past*.

"I'm in love."	He said he was in love.	Er sagte, er sei verliebt.
"We're happy."	They said that they were happy.	Sie sagten, sie seien glücklich.
"The flight goes at 9."	Jeff said the flight went at 9.	Jeff sagte, der Flug gehe um 9.

69 Einleitung in Vergangenheit: *Present Perfect* und *Past* werden zu *Past Perfect*.

"The profit has increased."	She said that the profit had increased.	Sie sagte, der Profit sei gestiegen.
"I saw Jim yesterday."	Sue told me she had seen Jim the day before.	Sue sagte mir, sie habe Jim am Tage zuvor gesehen.

70 Einleitung in Vergangenheit: *will* wird zu *would*, *can* zu *could* und *may* zu *might*.

"Will you marry me?"	Max asked Jill if she would marry him.	Max fragte Jill, ob sie ihn heiraten wolle.
"I cannot hear you."	Julie said she couldn't hear me.	Julie sagte, sie könne mich nicht hören.
"Ruth may arrive a bit late."	Her friend said Ruth might arrive a bit late."	Ihre Freundin sagte, Ruth komme vielleicht etwas später.

135 Drill indirekte Rede im Gegenwartssystem – Setzen Sie ein.

1 "We're happy." – "The Holdens say _____ happy."

2 "I'm hot." – "Pardon?" – "I'm hot and I've told you before that _____ hot."

3 "Mollie's ill." – "The doctor will confirm that Mollie _____ ill."

4 "I don't like bananas and I've told you a hundred times that I _____ like bananas".

5 "I get pains in my arm." – "Nick says he _____ arm."

6 "I often feel sick." – "Jane says that _____ sick."

136 Training indirekte Rede in der Erzählung – Passen Sie die Formen an.

1 "It's a beautiful day." – I heard Linda say _____ a beautiful day.

2 "Are you ready, Freddie?" – Eddie asked Freddie if he _____ ready.

3 "We have a new bed." – Mildred said _____ a new bed.

    ✺ Hören Sie die Reime, wenn Sie die ersten drei Lösungssätze laut lesen?

4 "I'm sure they will call." – Paul said he _____ sure that they _____.

5 "Chris often does the cooking." – Britta told us Chris _____ the cooking.

6 "You must see that film!" – Oliver was convinced that _____ that film.

7 "Did you see the show?" – Carol wanted to know if _____ the show. ✺

8 "I ate all the cookies." – Bob admitted that _____ all the cookies.

9 "You can stay if you want." – Barbara said _____ if I _____.

10 "My computer cost a lot." – Dan told me his computer _____ a lot.

11 "Susan? She may be at the office." – Bill said Susan _____ at the office.

12 "I'm flying to Egypt in April." – Michelle told us she _____ to Egypt in April.

13 "You sing well." – My teacher said _____ well."

14 "It's raining again." – Emily told me on the phone that _____ again.

15 "My bike has been stolen." – Geoff said his bike _____.

16 "I left home at 18." – Toni told me she _____ home at 18.

17 "George hasn't shaved." – I added that George _____.

18 "People won't notice." – Lucy thought that people _____.

19 "You don't need to worry." – I told Martina _____ worry.

20 "We're learning Spanish." – The boys said _____ Spanish.

21 "I did it yesterday." – Anna let me know that _____ it the day before.

Bedingungssätze Typ 3 _____ Conditional Clauses 3

Mit dem Third Conditional können Sie spekulieren, was gewesen wäre, wenn.
Die Sätze sind unreal, denn die Situationen sind schon vorbei.

71   Was passiert wäre, falls oder wenn

If we had booked earlier,	Bedingung	Wenn wir früher gebucht hätten,
we would have got good tickets.	Hauptsatz	hätten wir gute Karten bekommen.

(But we booked late and got bad tickets.)

I would have protested	Hauptsatz	Ich hätte protestiert,
if I had been there.	Bedingung	wenn ich dort gewesen wäre.

(But I wasn't there and I couldn't protest.)

WISSEN

- Im Hauptsatz steht would have + die dritte Form des Verbs.
  Im Bedingungssatz steht das Past Perfect, d. h. had + die dritte Form des Verbs.
- Verwenden Sie im Bedingungssatz kein would. Die Grundregel heißt:
  'if + would' is no good!
- Anstelle von would have gibt es für Möglichkeiten might have und für Fähigkeiten
  could have.

© Der Zeiten-Trainer, ISBN 978-3-9521442-3-7

72   Fähigkeiten und Möglichkeiten

Jane could have called you	Hauptsatz	Jane hätte dich anrufen können,
if she'd had your number.	Bedingung	wenn sie deine Nummer gehabt hätte.

(She couldn't call you because she didn't have your number.)

I might have passed	Hauptsatz	Ich hätte vielleicht bestanden,
if I had prepared better.	Bedingung	wenn ich mich besser vorbereitet hätte.

(I didn't pass because I didn't prepare well enough.)

I could have called you
if I'd had your number.

137 Training Bedingungssätze – Markieren Sie die richtige Form.

1   If I *would have been/had been* in your place, I *would have taken/would take* the job.

2   I *had travelled/would have travelled* to Bora-Bora if I *would have had/had had* the time.

3   What *would you have done/had you done* if you *hadn't had/wouldn't have* me to help you?

4   If it *hadn't/wouldn't have* rained, your garden party *would have/had* been a great success.

5   If Lisa *hadn't seen/wouldn't have seen* that car, she *might/had* have been killed.

6   I *would have bought/had bought* the house if I *had had/had* the money.

138 Training Bedingungssätze – Setzen Sie die beste Form ein.

1   If I (know) _____ you were back home, I would have called you.

2   You (not have) _____ that accident if you hadn't been drinking.

3   You might have won a million if you (buy) _____ a lottery ticket.

4   I would never have believed that if I (not see) _____ it with my own eyes.

5   Had I known that I would see you, I (shave) _____ of course.

6   If I had realised that the lights were red, I (stop) _____.

7   If you (tell) _____ me it was a secret, I wouldn't have said a word.

8   Of course I (give) _____ you a lift if I'd had a car.

139 Erzähltraining – Setzen Sie alle Formen ein.

1   If I (realise) _____ what a terrible driver she _____,
    I (never/go) _____ with her.

2   If I (know) _____ that you (be) _____ coming,
    I (buy) _____ some cookies.

3   Of course I (call) _____ the doctor immediately if she
    (say) _____ that she (have) _____ the pain
    for days.

4   If I (be) _____ told that the water (be) _____
    so cold, I (never/go) _____ swimming in the lake.

5   If Sue (send) _____ in her lottery ticket, she
    (may win) _____ a few million pounds.

6   If you (tell) _____ me that Max (be) _____ so
    hard of hearing, I (speak) _____ a bit louder and Max might
    (understand) _____ me.

140 **Testen Sie sich. Setzen Sie die besten Verbformen aus Unit 10 ein.**

1 When Lucy (arrive) _____ at the station, …

2 … the train (already/leave) _____.

3 Is Sue rich? – Well, she told me she (have) _____ €2 million in the bank.

4 Dean promised he _____ always be true to me.

5 I (know) _____ her for years …

6 … before we finally (go) _____ out together.

7 When Peggy (get) _____ back home yesterday, …

8 … she (realise) _____ that …

9 … she (leave) _____ her keys at the office.

10 George had a good plan, but he (not/know) _____ …

11 … whether it (work) _____.

12 Ann! I was just _____ call you myself.

13 What (you/do) _____ …

14 … when I (phone) _____ you yesterday?

15 Sam said he (be) _____ to Cuba many times.

16 When I asked Sally if Dan (be) _____ coming, …

17 … she said yes but he _____ be a bit late.

18 You came home yesterday? If I (know) _____ that …

19 … I (ask) _____ you round for dinner.

20 If Alex (marry) _____ Joan in 1991 …

21 … he (may) _____ become rich and happy.

22 If you (tell) _____ me that …

23 … Mollie (be) _____ so ill, …

24 … I (call) _____ an ambulance …

25 … and she (may be) _____ saved.

© Der Zeiten-Trainer, ISBN 978-3-9521442-3-7

141 Training Hilfsverben – Setzen Sie *am, are, is, was, were, do, does, did, will, won't* oder *used* in die Lücke.

1 Hi Lilly! _____ you all right? And how _____ your mother today?

2 That's a good offer. _____ you agree?

3 _____ Ben smoke? – Well, he _____ to, but he _____n't any more.

4 Oh, so you _____ at home last night. Why _____n't you answer the phone when I called? – Well, I _____ having a bath.

5 The play at the Theatre Royal last Friday _____ a success.

6 When _____ Elaine usually get up? – At 7.

7 _____ you call me when you get to Zurich?

8 We _____ have a financial problem unless they _____n't pay.

9 When I _____ walking home last night, I heard all these noises. – _____ you afraid? – No, I _____ never really afraid of the dark.

10 _____ you use to go jogging when you _____ a kid? – No, but we _____ to go skiing a lot. _____ you, too?

11 _____ you going to do the dishes? If so, I _____ give you a hand.

12 I _____ really very sorry. I promise I _____ do it again.

13 Hi Linda! It _____ George. Where exactly _____ you waiting for me?

14 Congratulations on your result! How _____ you do that?

15 What sort of books _____ you read?

16 How _____ you travel to work? – By train. I _____ to drive, but now there _____ just too much traffic.

17 What _____ you doing at 9.00 last night? – Why? _____ you try to call me?

18 I _____ going to learn Spanish. And when I speak it well enough, I _____ travel to Mexico.

19 Really? _____ you always do the shopping in the morning?

20 _____ there any cake left in the fridge? – Yes, but _____n't eat it all.

21 The fish, certainly, ma'am. And _____ you have a starter? – No, thanks, I _____. But I _____ have some dessert later.

22 _____ Maggie smoke? – No, but she _____ to smoke a lot!

23 _____ you enjoy this exercise? Or _____ it too long?

142 Training – Verneinen Sie die folgenden Ausdrücke.

1   Sharon wants to see you.   _____

2   We have lunch at 12.30.   _____

3   If you run, you'll catch the bus.   _____

4   Peggy's arrived.   _____

5   Bob's washing his car.   _____

6   Lloyd's got a lovely garden.   _____

7   The Pages went to Michigan.   _____

8   I'll have some rice.   _____

9   Cathy is going to study law.   _____

10 The manager agrees with the plan.   _____

11 We'd done it before the holiday.   _____

12 I'd call a doctor.   _____

13 Toby did the dishes.   _____

14 Chris put the milk in the fridge.   _____

143 Setzen Sie die passende Form von *do* ein.

1   _____ you watch the game last Monday?

2   That's terrible! What can we _____ now?

3   Hi Kelly! What are you _____ here in Stuttgart?

4   Nick went out for a beer after he had _____ all his homework.

5   We were _____ the shopping when we noticed a pickpocket behind us.

6   _____ Matthew like reading? – Yes, he enjoys it a lot.

7   I'm tired. I have been _____ too much work lately.

8   Has all the paperwork been _____ yet?

9   Good time to call! I've _____ everything and
    we could go out for a drink.

10 _____ you _____ all that work yesterday?
    Congratulations!

11 Do you want to _____ another exercise? –
    No thanks. That will _____ for now.

If you run,,
    you'll catch the bus.

144 Training Vorgegenwart oder Vergangenheit –
Wählen Sie.

1 I *have never been/never was* to India.

2 Thomas *has gone/went* to Nepal in 2003.

3 Yesterday I *didn't eat/haven't eaten* any lunch.

4 Vera and George *have already arranged/already arranged*
   their wedding.

5 When *did you start/have you started* learning English?

6 I *have recently met/recently met* Tim.

7 *Have you ever won/Did you ever win* anything?

8 When *were you/have you been* in China?

145 Training Vorgegenwart oder Vergangenheit – Setzen Sie ein.

1 This is the best film I (ever/see) _____.

2 How long (you/know) _____ Patricia?

3 When (you/meet) _____ her?

4 I (meet) _____ her in 2005.

5 (you/ever/be) _____ to Ireland?

6 Yes, I (go) _____ there last summer.

7 My sister (never/fly) _____ anywhere.

© Der Zeiten-Trainer, ISBN 978-3-9521442-3-7

146 Training Passiv – Setzen Sie die beste Form ein.

1 Fiat cars (make) _____ in Italy.

2 Spanish (not/speak) _____ only in Spain but also in other countries.

3 Last week Sonia's bike (steal) _____.

4 When is the next book going to (publish) _____?

5 The most valuable sunflowers (paint) _____ by Van Gogh.

6 The film ET (direct) _____ by Spielberg.

7 (you/ever/invite) _____ to a 5-star hotel?

8 A lot of mistakes could (avoid) _____.

9 They didn't realise that they were (watch) _____ by the police.

10 I was happy to see that the job (do) _____ while I was away.

Revision Units 1 – 10

147 **Training englische und deutsche Zeitformen – Übersetzen Sie.**

1   Was machst du heute Abend?   _____

2   Wie lange wartest du schon?   _____

3   Wann bist du eingetroffen?   _____

4   Wenn du mir hilfst,
    zahle ich das Nachtessen.   _____

5   Catherine mag keinen Fisch.   _____

6   Schau! Gleich regnet es.   _____

7   Der Zug fährt um 08.15.   _____

8   Tina! Was tust du hier in München? _____

9   Das Datum war geändert worden.   _____

10 Ich war froh,
    dass sie gekommen war.   _____

11 Früher rauchte ich.   _____

12 Sie brachen ein,
    während wir schliefen.   _____

13 Ich bin müde, weil
    ich zu viel gearbeitet habe.   _____

14 Mach' dir keine Sorgen.   _____

15 Nimm's locker.   _____

Schlusstest

Messen Sie Ihren Erfolg

Final Test & Evaluation of your Success

Unit 1

1   I'm afraid _____ are no tickets left.

2   Was _____ a good restaurant at the hotel you stayed in?

3   Yesterday _____ / _____ an antique market in our village.

4   _____ / _____ difficult to learn a new language.

5   How far _____ / _____ to the nearest post office?

6   _____ / _____ a lot of people at Bon Jovi's last concert.

7   ____ / _____ any ice-cream left? – No, we have eaten it all.

8   In August lots of shops _____ closed.

9   Last year we _____ in New York on business.

10 There _____ nothing interesting on TV last night.

Unit 2

11 What's the matter? Why (you/cry) _____?

12 PET bottles (not/belong) _____ in the normal garbage bin.

13 What (you/think) _____ of my new dress?

14 That can't be true. I (not/believe) _____ you.

15 Jimmy usually (wear) _____ a suit, …

16 … but today he (wear) _____ jeans.

17 Sarah! What (you/do) _____ here?

18 (you/not/like) _____ fish? I love it!

19 If you (want) _____ to understand this better, …

20 … you really (need) _____ to study harder.

Unit 3

21 I hope we (have) _____ the opportunity to see *Cats*.

22 Look at the sky! It (rain) _____ soon.

23 I don't think Valerie (marry) _____ Bernard.

24 Susan (have) _____ her second child next month.

25 We (have) _____ the steak, please.

26 What (you/do) _____ at the weekend?

27 Unless you (work) _____ harder, …

28 … you (not/pass) _____ this exam.

29 I (call) _____ you as soon as I get to New York.

30 Don't worry. I'm sure you (like) _____ the new boss.

Unit 4

31 Where (you/be) _____ at this time yesterday? …

32 … I (lie) _____ on a beach in Italy.

33 A hundred years ago people (work) _____ longer hours.

34 We (drive) _____ round a bend …

35 … when suddenly some cows (block) _____ the road.

36 Last Saturday there (be) _____ a thunderstorm.

37 As children we (ring) _____ door bells and then run away.

38 When (Marlis/move) _____ to Australia? – 10 years ago.

39 When I (wake up) _____ up this morning, …

40 … the sun (shine) _____.

Unit 5

41 If I (be) _____ you, …

42 … I (buy) _____ a new car.

43 _____ you like to pay by credit card? …

44 … No. I'd _____ to pay in cash.

45 _____ we watch the game tonight? – Yes, let's do that.

46 Buy a lottery ticket. You _____ win €3 million!

47 _____ you possibly drive me to the airport?

48 That box looks heavy. _____ me carry it for you.

49 I (not/work) _____ so much …

50 … if I (not/have to) _____ pay the rent.

Unit 6

51 You (look) _____ really good in those jeans.

52 Barbara (not/like) _____ skiing.

53 You can't come? But you (promise) _____!

54 He never (see) _____ my point of view.

55 What (you/think) _____ of Jim's new girlfriend?

56 (you/know) _____ Tony's wife?

57 (Thomas/still/have) _____ the same old car?

58 Yes, I (agree) _____ with you.

59 We (look) _____ at the menu …

60 … when Charles and Emily (come) _____ into the restaurant.

Unit 7

61   You _____ be exhausted after all this work.

62   I'm afraid I _____ help you.

63   _____ you please send me your latest price list?

64   I _____ work late yesterday.

65   If you're feeling that bad, you _____ see a doctor.

66   I hope I won't _____ make a speech at the wedding.

67   Sorry, I won't _____ to join you for lunch.

68   We _____ buy any more fruit as we have enough.

69   Yesterday we _____ to work. It was a bank holiday.

70   Were you _____ find out his address?

Unit 8

71   The light bulb (invent) _____ by Edison.

72   Last week the employees (inform) _____ about the changes.

73   Lunch (serve) _____ now.

74   At the border we (question) _____ by the customs officer.

75   This hotel can really (recommend) _____.

76   The new timetable (introduce) _____ on 1 May last year.

77   Joan (not invite) _____ to Joe's party last Saturday.

78   These cameras (not/manufacture) _____ anymore.

79   Where (your watch/make) _____?

80   A lot of cheese (produce) _____ in Switzerland.

Unit 9

81   How long (you) _____ living here?

82   We (never/be) _____ to Hawaii.

83   He (work) _____ hard all day.

84   (you/ever/eat) _____ sushi?

85   How are you? We (not/see) _____ each other for a long time!

86   Patricia (know) _____ Louis for a year.

87   Nobody (tell) _____ me about today's meeting.

88   Have the dishes (do) _____?

89   The letters (not/type) _____ yet.

90   How many cigarettes (you/smoke) _____ today?

Unit 10

91   When I (want) _____
     to get into my car, …

92   … I (realise) _____ …

93   … that I (forget) _____
     _____ my keys.

94   Last month they _____
     _____ married for 25 years.

95   There was no cake left, as
     we (eat) _____ it all.

96   If we had booked earlier, we
     (get) _____
     _____ better tickets.

97   I would have told you
     if I (know) _____
     where to reach you.

98   We (live) _____
     _____ in Berlin before we
     moved to Geneva.

99   I (send) _____
     _____ you an email
     if I had had your address.

100 He said he (be) _____
     very hungry so I made him
     a sandwich.

© Der Zeiten-Trainer

117

Der Business Korrespondenz Trainer

Englische Bürokommunikation, deutsch erklärt – E-Mail, Brief und Telefon

Das moderne Lernbuch für Business-Englisch mit der genialen ABCD-Methode: Jetzt endlich lernen Sie englisch texten, bis das Wesentliche sitzt – ganz einfach, aber von Grund auf. Sie brauchen nicht mehr Hunderte von Textbausteinen anzusehen, von denen doch keiner genau der richtige ist. Sie wissen auch, wie Ihre Briefe richtig tönen – durch Lesen, Hören, Schreiben.

✔ Super für Auszubildende, Kaufleute und Wiedereinsteiger/innen, als Lernbuch und als Nachschlagewerk

✔ Der Business-Korrespondenz-Trainer bringt Ihnen Sicherheit beim Texten von englischen Geschäftsbriefen

✔ Perfekt für individuelles Selbststudium und handlungsorientierten Unterricht

Ladenpreis	SFr. 38.80 / € 32,00
	132 Seiten plus CD und Beiheft
ISBN	978-3-952-1442-4-4

www.e-dito.ch
www.e-dito.de

Der Präpo·Trainer

Englische Präpositionen leicht gemacht – deutsch erklärt

Das echt starke Lernbuch für englische Präpositionen: Kurze, treffende Erklärungen werden ergänzt durch unzählige maßgeschneiderte Übungen. Der Präpo·Trainer spricht Sie an, ganz spontan. Sobald Sie das anregende Buch in den Händen halten, merken Sie, wie gut Ihnen diese Hilfe bei englischen Präpositionen tut.

Ladenpreis	SFr. 26.80 / € 22,30
	96 Seiten plus Lösungsheft
ISBN	978-3-9521442-2-0

Anhang

Verbformen
und
Zeitentabellen

Verb Forms
and
Tense Charts

Welche Verbform brauchen Sie für welche Zeitformen?

	Infinitiv	Vergangenheit	Partizip
	see	saw	seen
Present Simple	I **see** the problem.		
Nach do/doesn't	**Does** Joe **see** that?		
Present Continuous	**Are** you **seeing** Jenny tonight?		
Past Simple		Corina **saw** Jim at the party.	
Nach did/didn't	**Did** they **see** you?		
Present Perfect			Jack **has** never **seen** the Eiffel Tower.
will/won't **must/can't etc.**	Martha **won't see** you now. I **can't see** my glasses!		
if-Satz Typ 1	**If** you **see** Max, please tell him.		
if-Satz Typ 2		**If** Sue **saw** the point, she might come.	
if-Satz Typ 3			**If** we **had seen** Fred, we would have told you about that.
Passiv			The woman **was seen** at the airport. The Tower can **be seen** from here.

Wichtige unregelmäßige Verben _____ Irregular Verbs

Es folgt eine ziemlich umfassende Liste unregelmäßiger englischer Verbformen. Das Zeichen ᴿ nach der Grundform bedeutet, dass dieses Verb auch mit regelmäßigen Formen vorkommt. Ganz seltene Verben finden Sie in Wörterbüchern.

be (am, are, is)	was/were	been	sein
beat	beat	beat	(wiederholt) schlagen
become	became	become	werden
begin	began	begun	beginnen
bet	bet	bet	wetten
bite	bit	bitten	beißen
blow	blew	blown	blasen
break	broke	broken	(zer-)brechen
bring	brought	brought	bringen
build	built	built	bauen
burn ᴿ	burnt	burnt	(ver-)brennen
buy	bought	bought	kaufen
can	could	been able to	können, imstande sein
catch	caught	caught	fangen, erwischen
choose	chose	chosen	wählen
come	came	come	kommen
cost	cost	cost	kosten
cut	cut	cut	schneiden
deal	dealt	dealt	(aus-)teilen, handeln
dig	dug	dug	graben
do	did	done	tun, machen
draw	drew	drawn	ziehen, zeichnen
dream ᴿ	dreamt	dreamt	träumen
drink	drank	drunk	trinken
drive	drove	driven	treiben, Auto fahren
eat	ate	eaten	essen
fall	fell	fallen	fallen
feed	fed	fed	füttern
feel	felt	felt	(sich) fühlen
find	found	found	finden
flee	fled	fled	fliehen
fly	flew	flown	fliegen

121

forget	forgot	forgotten	vergessen
forgive	forgave	forgiven	vergeben
freeze	froze	frozen	(ge-)frieren
get	got	got	bekommen, werden etc.
give	gave	given	geben, schenken
go	went	gone	gehen
grow	grew	grown	wachsen, anbauen
have	had	had	haben etc.
hear	heard	heard	(an-)hören
hide	hid	hidden	(sich) verstecken
hit	hit	hit	treffen, schlagen
hold	held	held	halten
hurt	hurt	hurt	verletzen, weh tun
keep	kept	kept	(be-)halten, fortfahren
know	knew	known	wissen, kennen
lay	laid	laid	legen
lead	led	led	leiten, führen
learn [R]	learnt	learnt	lernen, erfahren
leave	left	left	abfahren, weggehen, verlassen
lend	lent	lent	leihen
let	let	let	(zu-)lassen
lie	lay	lain	liegen
lose	lost	lost	verlieren
make	made	made	machen, herstellen
mean	meant	meant	meinen, sagen wollen, bedeuten
meet	met	met	(sich) treffen
must	had to	had to	müssen
pay (for)	paid	paid	zahlen
put	put	put	legen, stellen, hintun
read	read	read	lesen
ride	rode	ridden	reiten, (mit-)fahren
ring	rang	rung	läuten
rise	rose	risen	sich erheben, steigen
run	ran	run	laufen, betreiben
say	said	said	sagen
see	saw	seen	sehen
sell	sold	sold	(sich) verkaufen

send	sent	sent	schicken, senden
set	set	set	setzen, einstellen
shake	shook	shaken	schütteln, zittern
shine	shone	shone	scheinen, glänzen
shoot	shot	shot	(er-)schießen
show [R]	showed	shown	zeigen
shut	shut	shut	(dicht) schließen
sing	sang	sung	singen
sink	sank	sunk	sinken
sit	sat	sat	sitzen
sleep	slept	slept	schlafen
slide	slid	slid	gleiten
speak	spoke	spoken	sprechen
spend	spent	spent	ausgeben, aufwenden, verbringen
spit	spat	spat	spucken, speien
spoil [R]	spoilt	spoilt	verderben, verwöhnen
spread	spread	spread	(aus-)breiten
stand	stood	stood	stehen
steal	stole	stolen	stehlen
stick	stuck	stuck	kleben, (hin-)stecken
strike	struck	struck	schlagen
swear	swore	sworn	schwören, fluchen
swim	swam	swum	(aktiv) schwimmen
take	took	taken	(auf-)nehmen, (hin-)bringen, Zeit brauchen
teach	taught	taught	lehren, beibringen
tear	tore	torn	reißen
tell	told	told	erzählen, sagen
think	thought	thought	denken, meinen
throw	threw	thrown	werfen
understand	understood	understood	verstehen
wake (up)	woke	woken	wecken, erwachen
wear	wore	worn	am Körper tragen
win	won	won	gewinnen
write	wrote	written	schreiben

Zeitentabelle, aktiv _____ Table of Tenses, active

Im Englischen hat jede Zeit zwei Aspekte resp. zwei Formen, die einfache Form und die Verlaufsform.

Bilden Sie die Verlaufsform mit be + –ing-Form des Hauptverbs.

Infinitiv → (to) write

Aspekt Aspect Zeit Tense	Einfache Form Simple	Verlaufsform Continuous
Zukunft Future	I will write	I will be writing
Vorzukunft Future Perfect	I will have written	I will have been writing
Gegenwart Present	I write	I am writing
Vorgegenwart Present Perfect	I have written	I have been writing
Vergangenheit Past	I wrote	I was writing
Vorvergangenheit Past Perfect	I had written	I had been writing
Konditional I Conditional I [1]	I would write	I would be writing
Konditional II Conditional II [2]	I would have written	I would have been writing

[1] Siehe Bedingungssätze Typ 2, S. 50
[2] Siehe Bedingungssätze Typ 3, S. 106

Zeitentabelle, passiv _____ Table of Tenses, passive

Bildung des Passivs: Setzen Sie be in die entsprechende Zeit und fügen Sie die
3. Form (past participle) des Hauptverbs an.
Damit die Tabelle übersichtlich und griffig bleibt, verzichten wir auf
ungebräuchliche Verlaufsformen.

Infinitiv → **(to) be written**

Aspekt Aspect	Einfache Form Simple			Verlaufsform Continuous		
Zeit Tense	Subjekt	**be**	3. Form	Subjekt	**be**	3. Form
Future	Mails	**will be**	written			
Future Perfect	Mails	**will have been**	written			
Present	Mails	**are**	written	Mails	**are being**	written
Present Perfect	Mails	**have been**	written			
Past	Mails	**were**	written	Mails	**were being**	written
Past Perfect	Mails	**had been**	written			
Conditional I	Mails	**would be**	written			
Conditional II	Mails	**would have been**	written			

Nach modalen Verben verwenden Sie den Infinitiv passiv

Mails	**can, could, may, might, should, must, will, would**	**be**	written
Mails	**are going to, have to**	**be**	written

Index

Der
Business
English
Trainer

Das wichtigste Englisch fürs Geschäft, deutsch erklärt –
Hören, Sprechen, Lesen, Schreiben.

Ein super Lernbuch für die wesentliche Sprache im Business. Einfach, verständlich und ohne unnötigen Ballast. Jetzt werden Sie sprachlich fit für den geschäftlichen Alltag in englischer Sprache, indem Sie die entscheidenden Fertigkeiten praxisnah schulen, bis sie sitzen. Telefonieren, Präsentationen, Sitzungen, Mails, Kundengespräch – lernen Sie, was Sie wirklich brauchen. Effizient, mit vielen hilfreichen Tipps!

✔ 12 kompakte zielorientierte Module für Hören, Sprechen, Lesen und Schreiben
   in den 12 wichtigsten Geschäftsangelegenheiten

✔ Anregendes Layout und durchdachte Auswahl der entscheidenden Sprachbausteine

✔ 95 abwechslungsreiche Übungen inklusive Lösungen und Skripts im Beiheft

✔ Solides modernes Lernkonzept mit CD zur Verstärkung

✔ Viele hilfreiche Tipps und Erfolgstests nach jedem Kapitel

✔ Ideal für Lernende ab zwei Jahren Englisch

✔ Für individuelles Selbststudium oder für den fixfertig vorbereiteten (handlungsorientierten)
   Klassenunterricht als Repetitions-, Auffrischungs- und Prüfungskurs

Der Business·English·Trainer
124 Seiten plus CD und Beiheft
ISBN 978-3-9521442-5-1
Preis Fr. 28.80/€ 24,00

www.e-dito.ch
www.e-dito.de

englisch
Grammatik

Grammatik deutsch erklärt – Englisch geübt

Dieses bewährte Werk ist die perfekte Ergänzung zu Kursen wie New Headway Elementary und Pre-Intermediate. Und mit diesen Selbstlern-Büchern erlangen Sie auf effizientem Weg und mit Vergnügen gute und solide Englisch-Kenntnisse. Mit über hundert genialen Übungen und Lösungsheft.

✔ Für individuelles Selbststudium oder Unterricht

✔ Besonders geeignet zum Auffrischen und Vertiefen Ihrer Englischkenntnisse

✔ Ideal als Ergänzung zu Kursen wie New Headway

✔ Der solide modulare Aufbau ermöglicht freies und gezieltes Lernen und Brush-up

✔ Die richtige Grundlage für Diplomkurse

✔ In praxisorientierter lebendiger Sprache

✔ Index und viele hilfreiche Lerntipps

✔ Klarer didaktischer Aufbau mit leicht verständlichen Erklärungen in Deutsch

✔ Starker Übungsteil inklusive separates Lösungsheft

Grammatik 1 (Elementary)
128 Seiten, mit Lösungsheft
ISBN 978-3-9521442-0-6

Grammatik 2 (Pre-Intermediate)
160 Seiten, mit Lösungsheft
ISBN 978-3-9521442-1-3

Die beste Ergänzung zu New Headway Elementary und New Headway Pre-Intermediate